I0786265

Third Edition

ISBN-13:
978-1725086685

ISBN-10:
1725086689

Artwork of both scripts by Rick C. Moore

DRAG411's Ten Black Books

Book 1:	**DRAG411's "DRAG Bully, A Survivor's Guide"** Copyright © 2015 and 2018
Book 2:	**DRAG411's "Original DRAG Handbook"** Copyright © 2010, 2011, 2012, 2014, and 2018
Book 3:	**DRAG411's "Crown Me! Winning Pageants"** Copyright © 2013, 2014, and 2018
Book 4:	**DRAG411's "DRAG King Guide"** Copyright © 2014 and 2018
Book 5:	**DRAG411's "DRAG Stories"** Copyright © 2011, 2014, and 2018
Book 6:	**DRAG411's "DRAG WYNTER, DRAG Father"** Copyright © 2012, 2014, and 2018
Book 7:	**DRAG411's "Spotlight Today"** Copyright © 2012 and 2018
Book 8:	**DRAG411's "DRAG Queen Guide"** Copyright © 2014 and 2018
Book 9:	Two Comedy Scripts: **DRAG411's "Best Said Dead"** Copyright © 2011, 2014, and 2018 **"Following Wynter"** Copyright © 2012, 2014, and 2018
Book 10:	**DRAG411's "DRAG World"** Copyright © 2012 and 2018

From the best-selling author of "CommUnity of Transition,"
"Two Days Past Dead," The Novel and the sequel,
"Turn Around Bright Eyes, The DRAG Queen Killer,"
"Joey Brooks, The Show Must Go On," and
"Waiting On God."

Best Said Dead

A Three-Act Comed

By Todd Kachinski Kottmeier
with Steve Hammond

Cast
[In order of Appearance]

All roles can be male, female, neither, or both!

Auggie Summers
A crime thriller writer accidently writes a bestselling drag queen book that takes over his home life. A boyfriend upset because Auggie is giving the drag community more attention, hits him in the head with a shovel. In ACT I, Auggie has blond hair wearing lederhosen.

Oliver Mason
Oliver is the curator of Auggie's imagination. Oliver comes across being very organized and authoritarian. Oliver wears the same clothes throughout play; white shirt, conservative dress pants with matching vest, dress shoes, and suit coat. .

Wynter Storm
Wynter is the reason people constantly forget thoughts in their mind. She always looks like she crawled out of bed, wearing in Act I through Act II, a rumpled robe [not white, since white conflicts with Serena's white choir robe]. The premise of Wynter, is this woman is actually pretty sloppy for someone claiming she is the only one that cleans. Wynter is very loud, and played over the top manic. Wynter Storm loves entertaining herself.

Little Victor Poom
Little Victor is played with accentuated sexuality by a flamboyant male. He often pushes boundaries of innocence in an attempt to steal attention and creates havoc in Auggie's mind. He wears a sexy little red outfit, in a devilish manner. It is wise to note, that only good memories can survive in Auggie's mind. Memories that did not hurt people flourish, while others vanished from Auggie's memory. Every sexually, dirty scene in the play is performed in comical effect, to show the hilarity of the innocence lost or tempted, more than for sexual conclusion.

Serena Silver
Serena is the no-nonsense moral character in your thoughts. In Act I, Serena wears a white robe and initially a halo (that she tears off her head, because she thinks the halo looks cheesy in Auggie's imagination). She never actually claims to be an angel. Serena represents the best of Auggie's thoughts. Serena is not considered funny by the other characters in the play. She dryly delivers the wittiest lines in the play. The spirit of Katharine Hepburn influences this character. After Act I, she is back to wearing normal clothes.

Act I ~ Scene One
Assuming APRON can hold four chairs with curtains closed.
APRON. Boxes represent a flat chair to resemble a bus seat.
A: Auggie   B: Elderly Women
C: Curtain open 3 ft. to exit bus

Act I ~ Scene One
Assuming APRON cannot hold four chairs with curtains closed.
Open curtain enough to place chairs. Ensure the chairs touch the right curtain to represent the bus wall. Leave a 3 ft. opening on the left of the chairs to represent the bus aisle.

Act I ~ Scene Two
Lights out. Curtain closed. May prerecord the dialogue to play it over speaker system.

The Stage

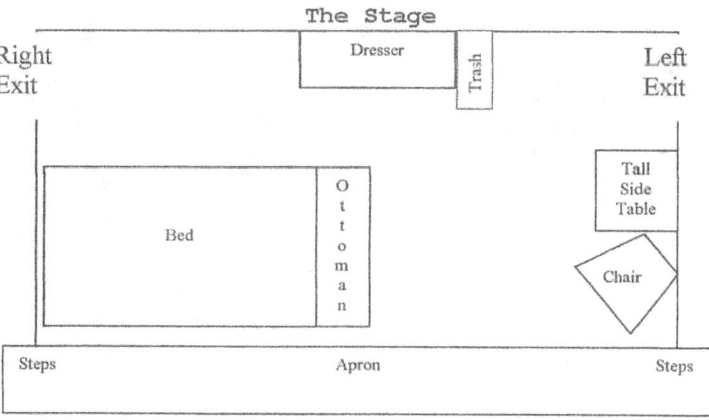

Preshow
Hand each audience member entering the auditorium a fuzzy ball. The pompom balls sold in most craft and dollar stores (Photo on page 8).

Act I ~ Scene One
The show will start with the curtains closed. The house and stage lights are off. Only a spotlight focuses on Auggie, as he sits on the left apron, on a bus seat. The seat next to him is empty.

ACT I ~ Scene Two

The emergency room scene in the start of ACT I has stage completely dark, until the vacuum noise begins. WYNTER turns on the vacuum, as the curtains open. Use the vacuum noise to hide the sound of the curtain.

Act I ~ Scene Three
[To end of play.]

See above staging.

Pom Poms
found in craft stores
(or find something equal)

“His whole life Auggie told people he was German.”

Act I BEST SAID DEAD
Scene One

Time: 3.00

> *Curtains closed. House and stage lights are off. Behind Auggie*
> *sits an elderly women staring at the red bandages on his head.*

AUGGIE: [*Auggie looks to his rear, over his left shoulder, in mid*
conversation.] ...no, no, no. I'll be alright

ELDERLY WOMEN: I don't know, I bet you'll need stitches. Did you fall
down some steps?

AUGGIE: No. I wasn't giving my boyfriend enough attention, so he cracked
me in the head with the neighbor's shovel, then took off in my car,
screaming at me, for at least three blocks.

ELDERLY WOMEN: Oh, I see. You're one of them.

AUGGIE: Gay?

ELDERLY WOMEN: No, a rude spouse. I had one of them for forty-nine
years. Buried him last year at Shady Acres.

AUGGIE: [*Trying to be witty.*] Was he still alive? [*Auggie smiles, but*
realizes smiling hurts his head.] Ouch.

ELDERLY WOMEN: That's what you get for trying to be fresh, young man.

AUGGIE: Sorry. [*Auggie pulls cord to stop bus.*]

ELDERLY WOMEN: Why didn't you call 9-1-1?

AUGGIE: No insurance, I'd be stuck with a bill. I decided to take this bus to
the walk-in clinic downtown, across from the bus terminal.

ELDERLY WOMEN: That is a serious cut to be taking on a bus. You barely
got on the bus without tipping over. [Pause.] Oh my dear, the blood is
pouring all down your neck now. Are you sure, you are all right son?

AUGGIE: I'll be okay. We're almost there.

ELDERLY WOMEN: So, [*Pause*] does your family know you're gay?

AUGGIE: Please, my mom joined PFLAG six months before I was born.

ELDERLY WOMEN: [*She scrunches her face.*] What's a "pee" flag?

AUGGIE: A support club for soccer moms and a few fathers with gay and lesbian children.

ELDERLY WOMEN: [*She suddenly pulls back her arms in surprise.*] You are bleeding hard now. I think I'm getting dizzy watching your blood drip down the back of the seat. I hope you're not going to die here, in front of me.

AUGGIE: Anyone can die. You can walk across the street and be hit by a bus. [*Auggie and the elderly women jerk forward, representing the bus stopping*]. Here's my stop. [Auggie exits stage. Pause. The elderly woman jumps up suddenly and screams.]

>	[*The lights instantly turn off, as you hear Auggie scream, followed by a half dozen other screams.*]

ELDERLY WOMEN: Oh my, that bus just ran over that dear boy. That man is mush!

>	Spotlight off. End of scene one.

Cassie and Victor during rehearsals

Oliver during the show

Act I BEST SAID DEAD
Scene Two

Time: 20.00

> *While the lights are off, pull the chairs off the stage. Auggie*
> *removes clothes he is wearing over German lederhosen. The cast*
> *and crew are screaming for help. As soon as the doctor says,*
> *"Auggie," the noises stop. The emergency room scene in the start*
> *of ACT I, Scene Two, is completely dark, with the curtains closed.*
> *You can hear the emergency room. You may want to pre-record*
> *this scene. Background noise should include a metal cart, busy*
> *room of voices, and a light humming of a flat-lined heart monitor.*

DOCTOR: Auggie! [*This word is the marker to stop all bus crash noise and switch to emergency room noise.*] Someone get the crash cart! Auggie, stay with us sport. [*The heart monitor has a solid tone.*]

AUGGIE: [*Solemnly.*] This is crazy. Why am I watching this doctor take care of me?

DOCTOR: Start CPR! Get respiratory in here now! [*Pause.*] Auggie, can you hear me?

AUGGIE: [*Getting a little frantic.*] Why can't any of you hear me? Crap. I've seen this before in movies, right after the person dies... Oh, crap.

DOCTOR: Has anyone called the lab? Give epinephrine, 1 mg, now! [*Pause. You can hear the commotion in the room. Suddenly the noises stop. Pause. Quietly.*] Okay, let's call it, time of death; 9:30.

[*Pause four seconds. Lights are still out.*]

OLIVER: Mr. Summers, Auggie Summers. [*Pause.*] Hello Mr. Summers. [*Pause.*] Are you all right Auggie?

AUGGIE: [*Almost in tears.*] Am I dead?

OLIVER: Yes, Mr. Summers, I'm pretty sure you already understand that you just died.

AUGGIE: Is this hell?

OLIVER: [*Laughs.*] No Mr. Summers, you didn't go to hell.

AUGGIE: [*Sounding relieved.*] Thank God. I'm in heaven!

OLIVER: [*Laughs again.*] Well not exactly Mr. Summers.

AUGGIE: I don't understand. Who are you?

OLIVER: Oh my, I apologize. I'm Oliver Mason... and don't call me Ollie.
Only my grandmother had permission to call me Ollie.

AUGGIE: Where am I Oliver?

OLIVER: You haven't gone anywhere. You're still in the place you have
always been, just now, you don't have a body to ride in.

AUGGIE: I'm confused. Are you saying, I didn't go to heaven?

OLIVER: Oh dear Mr. Summers, are you still religious?

AUGGIE: Yes.

OLIVER: Well, then you have to wait until judgment day. You will stay in
here, with only the positive memories created during your life.

AUGGIE: What happens to those that do not believe in God?

OLIVER: Nothing, same place as you. In their head, in their memories. It is
the bad people that regret dying, as their positive memories will be few.
They will be sick and tired of living the same memory over and over again,
knowing something is missing in their imagination.

AUGGIE: Where are you? Everything seems so dark in here. Do I get to
see you?

OLIVER: No Auggie. You forget eyes are those things, the body had in it.
Remember, all day long you walked around on Earth thinking, reasoning,
imagining, fantasizing, picturing people evaluating situations, and creating
game plans and goals?

AUGGIE: [*Unsure.*] Umm, ya.

OLIVER: You're in that place. We didn't go away. I'm the person that
decides in your life, which memories you kept, and which memories would
remain long after you died.

AUGGIE: Are you the reason I had a crappy memory when I was alive?

OLIVER: Don't be stupid Auggie! You can't abuse your brain and your body, and expect all of *us* to keep you on track.

AUGGIE: [*Caught off guard by the reference of the word, us.*] Us? So, you're not alone? I only hear your voice. Does this mean there are other voices in my head?

OLIVER: [*Laughs.*] Yes, Auggie. You are so funny. You know you have many voices and memories in your head. This is orientation, so it's just you and me. The past couple of weeks, I've been trying to get your memories in order. It's been a mess. I finally decided to dump most of your memories into three people: The good, the silly, and the wicked.

AUGGIE: The wicked? I thought only positive memories survived.

OLIVER: You can do wicked and silly stuff Auggie, without becoming a bad person. I believe your life began to define that path about ten years ago.

> [*A vacuum starts in the distance behind the closed curtains. Lights are still out. Curtains start to open. Auggie is sitting on the ottoman. Wynter is vacuuming in the dark. Oliver is still off stage.*]

OLIVER: Hello, Can you turn off the vacuum? We're working over here. [*The noise gets louder as brings the vacuum to the steps on LEFT CURTAIN.*]. Will you turn off that vacuum so I can talk to...

WYNTER: [*The vacuum instantly stops, Wynter interrupts Oliver.*] You will not raise your voice to me! You are not the boss of me. You told me three weeks ago that..

OLIVER: [*Interrupts Wynter.*] Auggie meet Wynter. [*Thunder claps; Stage lights turn on.*]

AUGGIE: Oh my Oliver! [*Auggie jumps to his feet.*] I thought you said I couldn't see people. I can clearly see Wynter. [*Auggie is noticing everything on stage. Auggie pulls himself away from Wynter, almost in fear, crossing to the center apron, looking for Oliver.*]

OLIVER: No. What you see is what your mind imagines Wynter to be...

AUGGIE: She's a drag queen! Why is my Wynter a drag queen?

WYNTER: [*Yells back at Auggie, offended by the comment*]. I'm not a damn drag queen. I'm a female impersonator!

AUGGIE: Why is my mother a female impersonator?

OLIVER: You created that memory Auggie, not us. I guess when you died; you were thinking more about drag queens, than your own mother.

WYNTER: I... AM... A... FEMALE... IMPERSONATOR. The next voice that calls me a drag queen, will be pulling this vacuum cleaner out of their butt!

AUGGIE: I don't mean to be freaking out, but it's not often a person dies.

OLIVER: What are you talking about Auggie? People die all the time. Some even get the chance to go back after they die.

AUGGIE: I want to go back!

WYNTER: Stop crying. You are so whiny.

OLIVER: You are in a better place Auggie.

AUGGIE: Never tell me I am in a better place. It cheats the life God gifted me.

WYNTER: Oh gosh, here the Auggie quotes start all over again.

AUGGIE: What do you mean by that comment?

WYNTER: [*Sarcastically repeats Auggie's quote.*] *Never tell me I'm in a better place. It cheats the life God gifted me.*

OLIVER: Auggie. Where do you think these quotes come from in your mind? Were you so gullible to believe you created the quotes yourself... were you?
 WYNTER: [*Laughs*] Were you?

AUGGIE: [*Points at WYNTER.*] Did you come up with that quote?

WYNTER: [*Laughs louder.*] Oh mercy no. Not my style. My job is to clean up this mess you call a mind. All day long, I have to scrub the clutter Victor flings into your imagination.

OLIVER: Serena put that quote in your mind. She is the voice in your imagination, reminding you of the man you wish to be in the world.

AUGGIE: What? Are you telling me, a female teaches me how to be the man I need to be?

WYNTER: Yes Auggie. That task is far too important to leave up to man.

AUGGIE: And what do you mean by Victor? I don't even know a Victor.

OLIVER: Sure you do. Victor is the imaginary twink you created to make fun of your friend Jason. He's been out of control ever since.

AUGGIE: Victor's not a real person. He's a make believe twink, created to tease Jason. I'd buy size 28 underpants, write Victor's name on the waistband, and sneak it into Jason's laundry.

OLIVER: That's the point I'm making. You created Victor in your imagination, and he took over. Victor convinced you to place that underwear in Jason's laundry.

AUGGIE: Did I ever have an original thought of my own?

WYNTER: Stop being a drama queen. You have tons of thoughts; just most of them were not actually functional in the real world.
OLIVER: Did you ever start talking and your friends looked at you like, "What are you talking about Auggie?"

AUGGIE: Sometimes.

OLIVER: *Those* were your thoughts.

WYNTER: I tried to erase them out of your head as fast as you created them, but you're so manic. Gibberish. I must have clogged three vacuum cleaners with your Gibberish.

OLIVER: Sometimes she would accidently clean too much and you would forget what you were doing. You know… go into a room; forget why you went in there. Start a sentence… forget the end of the thought. That type of stuff is WYNTER.

WYNTER: Hey, it's not my fault. Cleaning his imagination is like living with a hoarder.

AUGGIE: So was it WYNTER's fault that all the books I wrote were on different subjects with no focus? Who brought me all the crazy ones?

WYNTER: That dear, falls on you. You attract "crazy."

AUGGIE: All of this is driving me crazy.

WYNTER: Short drive!

OLIVER: Auggie! You need to focus on this orientation. None of us chooses when we get to be in here with you, and when we must leave.

AUGGIE: You leave?

OLIVER: We've always left during your entire life. You have many thoughts in your head, but never all of them at once.
AUGGIE: Are you sure? Many times, I felt confused.

WYNTER: That again, is my fault. Sometimes I vacuumed in the vacuum cord. Saw it sitting there on the floor, and ran it over just the same. [*Grabs vacuum handle. Wynter makes the noise with her mouth to imitate the cord choking in the brush, while bouncing the vacuum up and down in a wild manner.*].

OLIVER: [Interrupts WYNTER] As I said, Wynter tends to clean a little too much. You can always blame Wynter.

WYNTER: They often do. How Freudian.

OLIVER: [*Slowly says the phrase.*] You know Auggie, Tell me what you think, but I believe this sounds better…

AUGGIE: [*Thunder clap; Startled. Suddenly he can see Oliver.*] What just happened?

OLIVER: What do you mean?

AUGGIE: I can see you!

OLIVER: Good! It's about time you made me into somebody. Who am I?

AUGGIE: My editor. This is so creepy.

OLIVER: He looked creepy?

AUGGIE: No, he was a good-looking man. The way you said [*imitates the previous comment by Oliver*] "Well, you know Auggie, I believe my way is better."

OLIVER: [*To Auggie.*] I did not say, "I believe my way is better." [*To audience.*] At least, not with my outside voice. [*To Auggie.*] I'm glad you made me look like someone you actually liked. You have to be careful. Many of the people that irritated you in life could as easily have been the person you made me resemble. [*Auggie ponders the thought by pinching his chin.*] Try to think of people you enjoyed in life… you know, favorite teachers, heroes, even favorite movie stars.

      [*Lightning and thunder clasps; extended and loud, starts as lights start flickering like a strobe light.*]

WYNTER: Oh my Auggie, what have you done? [*Noise continues.*]

AUGGIE: [*Panics*] I don't know. Oliver told me to think of someone "I enjoyed thinking about."

OLIVER: [*Concerned, as the noise continues.*] I did not mean to say "enjoyed," I meant for you to pick the image of people in your mind carefully.

      [*Suddenly the noise stops. The lights turn off. The lights turn back on. On the bed is a flamboyantly dressed male in devil-red club kid gear, admiring himself.*]

VICTOR: I look fab-u-lus. Fabulous! Oh Auggie, I cannot believe I was in your mind. Look at me. I'm a sex kitten for e-ter-na-ty.

OLIVER: Oh my Auggie, what have you done?

WYNTER: [*Alarmed.*] He can't be in here! [*WYNTER starts hysterically running off stage, down the right apron staircase, into the audience. No eye contact with anyone off stage!*]

VICTOR: Cannot get rid of me now, you know the rules.

OLIVER: We cannot have Victor looking like this, Auggie. I said only good thoughts survive.
VICTOR: No, you didn't Ol-lie [*Sarcastically draws out the name "Ol-lie".*] You said thoughts survive as long as they don't hurt anyone.

WYNTER: [*Still screaming from RIGHT auditorium.*] I'm hurting, Wynter runs to LEFT auditorium.] I'm hurting!

VICTOR: Drama queen. I'm sitting over here on my bed. I'm not even touching you. Do you want to touch me Auggie? Finally, you can.

OLIVER: You won't talk like that in here.

WYNTER: Make him shut up Auggie!

AUGGIE: I can't make him shut up.

OLIVER: It's your mind. If you concentrate enough, you can block Victor out.

VICTOR: I will keep popping back up over and over again. You have no choice. Oliver stuck all your memories into a handful of people. I hold a large quantity of your life inside of me. Are you willing to sacrifice, for eternity, all the memories I hold?

OLIVER: This is going to be messy Auggie.

WYNTER: I am not cleaning this up Oliver. This is your mess.

OLIVER: I didn't make this mess. Blame Auggie!

AUGGIE: How can you blame me? Nobody gave me a rulebook ten minutes ago.

VICTOR: Why are all you old people freaking out? I'm not in here to take away your social security checks. If anyone asks, I am a Democrat, part of those ninety-nine percenters. I'm what's "in" now.

WYNTER: I can tell by looking at Victor that he will be trouble.

AUGGIE: You are Victor?

VICTOR: Oh, yes Auggie. Victor Poom.

WYNTER: Concentrate Auggie. Make him go away. *[Wynter runs back on stage.]*

OLIVER: You can concentrate Auggie, concentrate. Concentrate. CONCENTRATE.

VICTOR: [*Sarcastically.*] Yes, Auggie con-cen-trate. Concentrate on all those things that made you giggle in life. Concentrate on how adorable I look in these tight leather pants with this ripped body, and fab-u-lus smile.

OLIVER: [*Yells at Victor*] Shut up Victor.

WYNTER: I won't have this kind of talk in this room. My hair hurts!
[Wynter is holding the curlers in her hair, as if they are pulling out. She continues to circle the stage.]

VICTOR: [*Continues to instigate Oliver and Wynter.*] Concentrate, con-cen-trate. Oh my Auggie, I am so adorable. A-dor-a-ble.

[*A low key vibrating begins*]

VICTOR: [*Screams*] Oh dear!

WYNTER: What is that vibrating noise?

[*The noise gets louder, and Victor's laughter becomes more hysterical.*]

OLIVER: [*To Auggie.*] Auggie, what have you done?

WYNTER: I can't tell where the vibrating noise is coming from... it's everywhere!
AUGGIE: I didn't mean to think about it.

OLIVER: About what?

[*The vibrator noise gets louder.*]

OLIVER: About what?

WYNTER: [*Wynter looks upstage next to bed. The sheets on the bed block the view.*] What is that on the floor, next to the bed? Oliver, get that out of here!

OLIVER: [*Oliver looks at toy.*] Victor! What have you done? We can't have those kinds of toys in here!

WYNTER: It's contraband!

AUGGIE: I am sorry, I am sorry. I don't know what to say.

WYNTER: I refuse to touch it!

AUGGIE: I am sorry. I didn't know.

OLIVER: I... will... have... order in here. We will not have this behavior on my watch.

WYNTER: Are you kidding me? It's wet! EEEEEEW! [*She screams*]

VICTOR: It is not wet Wynter, it's slimy! [*Victor cannot stop laughing, which has Auggie giggling.*]

WYNTER: Don't start laughing Auggie!

AUGGIE: [*Giggling to Auggie.*] I can't help myself. You make me giggle. I so remember you now, inside of my head, when I was alive.

VICTOR: Auggie, is it yours baby?
AUGGIE: It is not mine!

OLIVER: Only you can create objects in your mind!

WYNTER: Stop thinking about it …it's growing!

OLIVER: What do you mean, "It's growing?"

VICTOR: It is starting to move!

      [*Wynter runs over to the chair next to the table and stands on it.*]

WYNTER: This is not funny. I blame you Victor!

VICTOR: [*To WYNTER.*] Why me? Get off that chair before you break something. I never owned one of those types of toys. I'm just a figment of Auggie's twisted imagination. [*To Auggie*] Make it move Tiger, make it move!

OLIVER: Shut up Victor!

VICTOR: Make it move. Make it crawl across the floor to Wynter. [*Victor holds both hands together to imitate jaws snapping at Wynter. [He growls and makes snapping noises. Auggie begins laughing harder.*]

WYNTER: [*Screams.*] This is not funny at all!

VICTOR: Oh yes it is!

      [*Suddenly the noise stops, at the same second, the entire cast stops making noise. This will show the effect of sudden silence. All the actors are looking at each other. Victor is looking next to the bed, but it is no longer in sight. Victor gets off the bed upper stage, and crawls under the bed to look for the missing noise.*]

OLIVER: [*Voices relieved.*] Thank you Auggie.

WYNTER: Still not funny. [*Wynter gets off the chair. She looks cautiously towards the bed.*] Do not do it again Auggie!

AUGGIE: I don't know what I did to create it. I'm dead, and my greatest fears of wondering if I was crazy are being answered in the most Tim Burton meets Dr. Seuss, kind of way.

VICTOR: [Looks under bed.] So Oliver, where's the contraband?

OLIVER: What were you thinking Auggie, moments before it vanished?

VICTOR: Yes Auggie, re-think it, bring it back.

AUGGIE: [*Ignores Victor.*] I don't know. I felt guilty.

VICTOR: Guilty? It didn't hurt anyone. You can be a sexual Auggie and not be a bad person.

WYNTER: You cannot tell me that this did not hurt someone. It hurt my feelings; it made me feel bad.

AUGGIE: Exactly. That is exactly what I thought. I felt guilty for upsetting you.

VICTOR: Wynter made him feel guilty?

WYNTER: Good, he should feel guilty. I was very upset.

OLIVER: No, it wasn't Wynter.

WYNTER: Yes it was Oliver, I felt bad.

OLIVER: You don't have that power over Auggie's imagination.
WYNTER: [Sighs, let down.] Oliver is right. That's why Oliver and I couldn't stop him from manipulating your imagination. Victor's like a cute little devil on your shoulder whispering in your ear.

VICTOR: Unfair! Well, except for the I'm cute and adorable part. Why if Wynter convinces him to clean his room, it is called, "convincing," yet everything I do is called manipulation.

OLIVER: [*Yells loudly around the room.*] Serena Silver? Serena?

WYNTER: Do you think Serena is here?

AUGGIE: Who is Serena? [*Auggie is now standing next to Oliver, following Oliver's line of sight.*]

WYNTER: Auggie. It is really important that you think hard before creating the appearance of Serena!

> [*Oliver and Auggie move towards lower center stage facing the audience. WYNTER takes a seat at the desk. Victor gets back on his bed, but this time he places the sheet partially over himself.*]

OLIVER: Serena, I know you are in here. [*Looks into the audience.*] Serena!

WYNTER: Don't look out there, I promise there is only trouble lurking in that field of corn.

VICTOR: I am not sure I'm prepared for Serena. [*Victor sits the pillow on his lap. He is insecure; no longer laughing.*] Do not call her; she is a do-gooder. They drive me crazy with all their rules. Maybe she went away.

OLIVER: [*Glances up.*] Serena?

AUGGIE: [*Follows Oliver's line of sight to the ceiling*] Is she an angel? [Short single thunderclap. Lights off. Lights on.]

> [*A loud voice bellows from the back stage. You cannot see Serena, but hear her voice yelling.*]

SERENA: [Screaming off stage.] Oh hell no! Are... you... kidding... me. This is redundant. I look like Annie Lennox at a Lilith Fair concert. Hello, Can we spell cliché?

AUGGIE: Who is that voice? Is that Serena?

WYNTER: [*Yells in the direction of the voice.*] I can spell cliché.

OLIVER: Wynter, hush. Don't get her started. You know Serena has no sense of humor.
> [*In walks Serena. Victor quickly tosses the sheet over himself like a sail, catching the attention of Serena. Serena is wearing a choir robe with a very used, feathered halo. She walks like a trucker and speaks with a raspy woman's voice.*]

SERENA: I have a sense of humor; it's just none of you clowns are funny. Now Katherine Hepburn, she was funny. [*Serena walks over to the sheet on the bed hiding Victor. Yells loudly.*] You in their Poom?

[*Victor's sheets start shaking violently.*]

VICTOR: [*In a high-pitched voice.*] Yes ma'am, PLEASE don't hurt me!

SERENA: [*Looks slowly at Wynter, checks her up and down. She looks at Oliver, checks him up and down. Grabs the blanket over Victor, yanks it off the bed.*] Boo!
SERENA: [*Victor lets out a large scream. Serena looks at the bed sheets, at Victor's feet, then over to Wynter.*] I hope you're going to make him clean up that puddle.

OLIVER: Well, we now know how you pictured Serena.

AUGGIE: [*Defensively.*] You looked up. I thought she was God, or an angel. [Serena crosses over to Auggie; places her face about a foot from his face.]

SERENA: Look at us. Is this the best of your imagination? [*Serena reaches up, tears off the halo on her head. Auggie smiles.*] This goes first. It makes my head itch. It looks like a Goodwill party prop for Halloween. Do you think this is funny?

AUGGIE: No! Well, a little... I never pictured my angel as a lesbian.

SERENA: [*Bobs her head.*] Excuse me, I DISTINCTLY heard Oliver explain to you that the good in you was because of me, a woman. He told you, the task is far too important to leave up to a man.

VICTOR: I think you look pretty.

SERENA: [*Ignores Victor.*] Why are you dressed in lederhosen?

WYNTER: I did that, because his whole life Auggie told people he is German.

VICTOR: His whole life he told people he was a Scorpio.

OLIVER, AUGGIE, SERENA, and WYNTER: [*In Harmony.*] Shut up Victor!

SERENA: Why is his hair yellow?

OLIVER: It's natural blond.

WYNTER: No, it's not; it's orange.

VICTOR: His hair is naturally blond. Auggie still has the L'Oreal box to prove it.

SERENA: [*Sits on the ottoman.*] It is going to be a long time, stuck in here with all of you.

WYNTER: Oliver, I blame you for all of this… [*Wynter points to the audience.*] Look at them.

OLIVER: [*To Serena.*] You told him, and I quote, "Run through life for there is plenty of time to rest at the end." [*Oliver points at audience.*] This is what you get when you live a rich life, of incredible memories.

VICTOR: That is a nice life motto. "Run through life for there is plenty of time to rest at the end."

OLIVER: [*Sits down on the end of the bed.*] Yes, but some of this [*Points again at the audience.*] is also the result of living life with reckless abandonment.

AUGGIE: Am I supposed to be doing something right now?

VICTOR: You can cheat and remember more fun memories.

SERENA: Please, Auggie does not cheat well.

VICTOR: I helped him cheat his sister playing Monopoly.

AUGGIE: She still won.

WYNTER: She was a better player.

OLIVER: She cheated better than you did.

SERENA: Crime never pays off in the end.

VICTOR: It does if you are smart.

OLIVER: They fill prisons with people smarter than the law.

WYNTER: [*To Auggie.*] I can't believe you went to church.

AUGGIE: Could you imagine how bad I would be without it

WYNTER: You were always in trouble.

AUGGIE: I didn't look for trouble. It found me.

WYNTER: Blame Victor.

SERENA: You can only blame yourself. People are so quick to blame other people for their problems. Only you ultimately control your life. Victor's a reflection of you. The worse you got, the stronger he became.

OLIVER: And the stronger he became the worst you got. Frick and Frack, one playing off the other.

AUGGIE: I made many good choices too. Do they reflect anywhere in here?

VICTOR: [*Sarcastically.*] Yes that explains why Serena is more butch than me.

> [*Serena Stands. Victor jumps to the floor and hides behind the bed on the floor.*]

WYNTER: I'm out of here. I smell blood in the water! [*Grabs the vacuum and exits STAGE LEFT.*]

[*Serena starts to exit stage. She walks over to the bed and pulls Victor out by the foot, and proceeds to exit the stage with Victor screaming.*]

VICTOR: I said you were pretty! I said you were pretty! I said you were pretty!

> [*Auggie stands. Oliver stands, walks over to Auggie and sits him back down.*]

OLIVER: It's best you just sit here Auggie.

OLIVER: [*looks at the audience, grimaces, nods his head in disapproval.*] This is going to take some time, and it's not going to be pretty.

Lights turn off. End of Act I

"...focused on the flaws, focused on the flaws."

Act II: Best Said Dead
Scene One

Time: 8.00

> *Only Wynter and Serena are in the room. Wynter is making the bed, while walking around the whole time holding a small pile of sheets. Serena walks around the room. Does nothing to assist Wynter.*

WYNTER: Constantly cleaning. Of all the people in his mind, why did they choose me to clean? From the moment I wake up until the moment I close my eyes, I am cleaning. [*Wynter kicks the pizza box under the bed.*]

SERENA: [Rolls her eyes.] I am sure, adjusting the mess from one side of Auggie's imagination to the other, does not qualify as cleaning. [Serena watches Wynter pick up the two shoes, tossing them into the garbage can. Serena stands, walks to the trash, removes the shoes, and neatly places them next to the bed.]

WYNTER: You're right. It is not that I can't clean it up. The point is, his life created so many memories. Much of this I blame on you.

SERENA: Why me?

WYNTER: You told Auggie to live his life with the imagination of his youth.

SERENA: You make his mind sound over-crowded.

WYNTER: It is Serena. Auggie's thoughts are like Star Trek Tribbles. Fuzzy balls of puff, falling into my hair each time I open a cupboard or closet.

SERENA: Drama! That is all you are Wynter Storm. You should be the first to know that Victor removed all the closets out of here two decades ago.

WYNTER: [*Looks at Serena, as if the point is obvious.*] I need to make room. Oliver collects too many sad thoughts.

SERENA: You need bad memories to define happiness. If you go through life with a gold spoon in your mouth, you will never appreciate the people around you. You will assume people should treat you well, without anything in return.

WYNTER: [Pauses to think of statement.] I obsess about people thinking I am a failure.

SERENA: I always told Auggie, "Every second you waste on someone with
no faith in you, YOU [Points at Wynter] steal from others that do…"

WYNTER: Many people are sad because they ruined their lives, and one
day they wake up, too old to change.

SERENA: You are never too old to renovate your life. The people that feel
their lives are nothing fail to look at the details. The happiness is in the
details. Tomorrow's best changes began yesterday. Failure is often your
self-conscious setting you up for a better reward.

WYNTER: People create rumors.

SERENA: Never confuse creating rumors, with creating life. Perceptions of
how you view yourself starts in here. [*Serena points to her own head.*]
Many times they're wrong. Perception of convenience is the part of your
rationale that convinces you that a YIELD traffic sign is yellow when it's
actually always been red.

WYNTER: [*Looks confused.*] But, a yield sign is yellow.

SERENA: No WYNTER, it has always been red.

WYNTER: In my neighborhood, they were yellow.

SERENA: That's the point I'm trying to make. Your mind plays tricks on
you. The yield signs have never been yellow. If you're a bad person and
desire to become a good person, you need to block out all the voices
reminding you, "it's hard to be good, when it's so easy to be bad."

WYNTER: But people won't let me change. They guilt me to change, but
once I start, they never forget to remind me that I am bad.

SERENA: Because you are listening to the wrong people.

WYNTER: [*Stand.*] I see myself better than this. [Wynter uses her hands to
point at her hair rollers and robe.] You are right, I let others in here tell me
the type of person I am supposed to be. [*Wynter walks to the dresser to
open the drawer, to replace the sheets in her arms. Inside the drawer, she
pulls out a dozen fuzzy balls, which resemble the balls we handed the
audience.*] Tribbles! [*Wynter throws them into the audience.*]

SERENA: [*Stands crossing over to the table.*] They are not Tribbles. They
are TAGS. [*Serena removes a few from a basket on the table, placing one
in Wynter's hand.*}

WYNTER: [*Puzzled.*] I don't understand.

SERENA: [*Walks downstage. Serena is holding a sole fuzzy ball in the tips of her hand, a few inches from her face.*] A TAG, to tag a memory.

WYNTER: [*WYNTER empties drawer of the balls to top of the dresser, so she can place the clothes back into the drawer.*] Why are there a million of these TAGS all over Auggie's imagination? Did I miss something from his life? Is this a hoarder thing? I saw an episode on hoarders one night on 60 Minutes. It got me quite ill.

SERENA: No. No, not at all. I told Auggie to go to the craft store and buy a giant bag of colored fuzzy balls for a dollar. I told him to go to the thrift store to find the most beautiful clear glass vase he could find. Each night he was to place one single ball into the vase, to represent one single thought that was positive that day.

WYNTER: What defines a positive thought?

SERENA: Anything. A clerk at the store that went out of her way to take care of him, a nice smile shared by a waiter, perhaps a call from a family member, or a note from a friend...

WYNTER: Only one fuzzy ball per memory?

SERENA: Very simple. Just one. Place it in the vase. [*Serena places the ball in the vase.*]

WYNTER: Did Auggie think it was stupid?

SERENA: Very stupid, until one day he was feeling depressed, sitting on his couch, watching *Pricilla, Queen of the Desert.* Auggie noticed the fuzzy balls in the bowl, representing hundreds of memories of life being good.

WYNTER: [*Now understands the revelation.*] A Tag; Auggie tagged a good moment with one of those balls. I get it. [*Wynter crams the last of the sheets into the dresser.*] I have a plan for changing my life. Can you help? [*WYNTER starts to pull Serena off STAGE LEFT.*]

SERENA: Not like, I am going anywhere else anymore.

> [*The two women start to leave the stage. Wynter has now made a reluctant friend in Serena. Wynter reaches over to grab her hand, almost skipping off stage, towing Serena.*}

WYNTER: Oh, this is going to be so much fun. [*Walking backwards, pulling Serena towards the exit. Serena resists*] I can't believe we never got together before. I have so many plans of stuff we can do. Does Auggie have a memory in here, of... a mall?

       [*Serena and Wynter exit stage. Pause. Victor and Auggie enter in
       mid-sentence STAGE RIGHT. Auggie now wears normal clothes.*]

VICTOR: ...now don't get me wrong Auggie. I am the first person to tell you I push the line. I have to Auggie. You are a nerd! You have always been a nerd, and not one of those [*Victor uses his index and second fingers of each hand, to punctuate the quotation marks.*] "honor's club in high school" nerds, but one of those, "Oh my god, Auggie's a dork" nerd.

AUGGIE: Are you always going to be mean to me?

VICTOR: [*Suddenly reaches to Auggie to stop him. Victor is very serious.*] Please Auggie. Please tell me you did not believe all your own hype about being popular. Please tell me you knew since high school, that you were a poser.

Auggie: {*Auggie tries defending himself.*] I was not totally out of the loop. Everyone knew my name.

VICTOR: Six billion people on the planet know the name gonorrhea, but you never heard one of them exclaim, "Gosh, gonorrhea seems pretty popular today." [*Victor changes his voice, mocking Auggie by pretending to be several people.*] "Oh, if I could only get me some of that gonorrhea for my birthday", "Ma'am can I get you some of that gonorrhea. IT'S THE RAGE ON BROADWAY, you know?"

AUGGIE: [*Defensively, almost mad.*] I have never heard of you Victor Poom until I died last week.

VICTOR: [*Laughs.*] Oh dear man of simple ideas. EVERYONE has heard of me. Do you think I only sat on YOUR left shoulder in life? Please. [*Speaks to audience.*] I am every little whisper, in every single person's imagination, that giggles to say... [*Reassuringly.*] "Go ahead honey. It is all right. I won't tell! [*Burst into laughter.*] When you moved back to be near your family, they settled you down. What was it your friend said, when he asked if the Infamous Auggie had returned?

AUGGIE: [*Auggie rolls eyes.*] Only in storybook form my friend, only in storybook form. I had enough of your help when I was alive. I need to make God know I am a good person.

VICTOR: There is nothing that you can teach God. He knew you, before you knew yourself. I believe God wants you to follow the right path in life, because it is the right path, not because you feel guilty.

AUGGIE: So you do represent good too. I'm so confused. Why are you dressed like the devil?

VICTOR: You dressed me this way tiger. Plus, when you moved back, I thought you'd be more frisky. You wrote that adorable dating profile, and I thought... job security.

AUGGIE: Which dating profile?

VICTOR: [*Victor pretends to mock Auggie by writing in the air.*] "I decided to return home once again after discovering there were many more innocents to corrupt. I... apologize... for my absence... and will do my best... to fulfill my bad... boy... [*Victor points to himself in ownership of the phrase.*] ...obligations; to keep my reputation intact."

AUGGIE: I was trying to be clever, perhaps even witty.

VICTOR: Auggie, you were always trouble. Even your sisters and brother begged your parents to say you were adopted.

AUGGIE: I'm sure most of them still do! So, have you seen God?

> [*Oliver enters the room. He is carrying a clipboard. Oliver looks around, checking off a list that is contained on the board.*]

VICTOR: I only felt God, because you felt God. You do not understand this concept of your death. If you struggle in here to find God, it is because you never placed God inside of you.

OLIVER: Great! Just what we need, advice from Victor on behaving.

AUGGIE: Actually, I am stunned learning he is not "*all bad.*"

VICTOR: Don't wave that phrase around. In here, bad is all I have...

OLIVER: That was Victor's master plan. To make you a bad boy. It looked ridiculous on you. Talk about over-selling!

VICTOR: Don't listen to him Auggie. You pulled it off well.

OLIVER: Yeah, as well as Capri pants. Victor, take him over to Serena's place.

VICTOR: Serena is scary. Why me?

OLIVER: Do you see anyone else I could possibly be speaking to Poom?

VICTOR: [Points to the audience.] Make one of them, out there.

OLIVER: [Points to the back left exit from upper stage.] Get out of here right now. I'm tired of all this grief. I should not have to tolerate this from a "BOY" your age. My neckties are older than you are!

VICTOR: [Sarcastically.] No argument there. We've seen your neckties. [Oliver glares at Victor, who leaves the stage with Auggie in tow]

OLIVER: [*Walks to the center of the apron, facing the audience.*] It has been awhile since we all sat down and spoke to each other. Now, before you all start talking at once, I have something to say. [*Pause, looking around the room. Seems to be counting people.*] Gosh. I never realized that so many late arrivals came in before Auggie died. Yes, yes. I know, most of you have a very blank expression on your face. Okay, a few of you seem lost. [*Oliver looks at one person in particular.*] Especially you. What? Oh, I'm sorry. [*Oliver looks towards the other side of the room.*] For some, the look is just natural, too natural. [*Pretends someone from the back of the room, asked a question.*] I'm sorry. I don't understand your question. [*Trying to repeat the woman's question to the rest of the audience.*] She left the house... thinking she was heading to a play and wound up here. [*To the woman.*] Sorry ma'am. You didn't make it. You are only a memory in Auggie's imagination. [*To the rest of the audience.*] If you are here because you thought you were heading to a play this evening, you are mistaken. Each of you represents a memory in Auggie's head. [*Oliver pulls out one of the small fuzzy balls the audience received earlier.*] If you have one of these TAGS, you are a cherished memory. Some of you are childhood thoughts, many of you are dreams. [*Oliver continues to glance across the room.*] Goals. Moments in time. Christmas. Puppies. A teacher's good grade. Graduation. The feeling a person gets when a newborn child reaches up to grasp a single finger for the first time. Most people run through life without inventorying the incredible moments that created the happiness in their own lives. If they did, they would be happier people, on a happier path, purposely creating happier circumstances. [*Oliver looks at the fuzzy ball a little closer.*] Sadly, few people understand that happiness is truly in the details of their life. They are constantly chasing the greener grass on the other side of the fence. Most are oblivious. Often, the greener grass on the other side of the fence is just healthy weeds. [*Oliver heads to the dresser, opens the drawer, pulls out a hand full of fuzzy balls.*] [Tossing one fuzzy ball into the audience with each word "one"] One, by one, by one, by one… people place those tiny moments of their lives in storage. [*Oliver holds his hands out to show the balls to the audience.*] They forget about the laughter people shared. They forget about the smiles, the hugs, the unconditional trust people gave them during their lives. [*Oliver walks over to the dresser and tosses the fuzzy balls into the bowl.*] People do not appreciate their lives. They spend so much time demanding constant attention that rarely time is spent cultivating the incredible life God gave them. [*Oliver prepares to leave the stage.*] I once saw a room of people, staring blankly at a black shoe smudge someone had placed on a beautifully painted wall. More attention was spent talking about the flaw than was shared with the artist that spent three days brush stroking the mural. So many people complain because others discount them for their flaws without taking into consideration their strengths. These are often the same people that discount their own lives. They ignore the great moments of their own lives, because they are so focused on the flaws. [Walking off the stage, hesitates, looks back into the audience.] Focused on the flaws…

Lights turn off. End of Act II

INTERMISSION

Act III: Best Said Dead

Scene One

Time: 4.00

> *Curtain remains closed. Wynter and Auggie enter in mid-sentence STAGE LEFT, in front of the CURTAIN on the LEFT APRON. WYNTER is dressed beautifully. Her hair is styled nicely, make up perfect, and wears a pretty dress.*

AUGGIE: So the shovel didn't kill me? I don't know. Manny hit me pretty hard with the neighbor's shovel.

WYNTER: Too funny. Actually, you made it to the bus stop across from the hospital. You stumbled out of the bus, lost your balance, just in time to fall off the sidewalk, in front of the very same bus. [*Wynter imitates in exaggeration the sounds.*] Crunch, creak, crunch, mush. The driver heard the crunching, slammed the breaks on, bringing the entire bus, to rest on top your chest. [*Pauses.*] Now that must have left a mark. Took them hours to figure out the plan, to untangle your legs from the wheel well of the bus.

AUGGIE: [*Auggie grabs his chest.*] Glad I don't have that memory. I never realized that busses killed so many people.

WYNTER: Sure you did, why do you think so many people walk around stating, "anyone could die from walking across the street and being hit by a bus." Those drivers are looking to hit people. They're crazy that way. [*Wynter again imitates in exaggeration the sounds.*] Crunch, creak, crunch, mush. Boom! Boom! Two points for driver! Twelve for the week! Boom! Boom! Boom! [*Whispers to Auggiein a conspiratorial voice.*]

They count you know. That is where the driving term comes from. You know, "Hit it in the road, two points. Four points if it's still alive." Police hide those statistics, part of the game.

AUGGIE: [*Nodding his head in disbelief of Wynter's crazy observation.*] I doubt he hit me on purpose. People are not that off kilter.

WYNTER: Are you kidding me? They are doing stuff like this all day long. You can't trust people. I am not stating they are all bad ALL THE TIME, just be careful because... [*Wynter is interrupted by Serena entering STAGE RIGHT. Wynter and Auggie Stop CENTER STAGE on the apron. Serena approaches Auggie.*]

SERENA: Auggie. Don't listen to her babble. Wynter is jaded. How ridiculous. Blaming the next person for something the previous person did to you. It is not the new person's fault you have incredibly poor judgment.

WYNTER: Toxic people are attracted to people wearing their hearts on their sleeves. Auggie, you will get hurt. Do you want emotional scars?

AUGGIE: I would rather go through life hurt by the few people that try to use me, than to go through life hurting innocent people. I always knew I wanted to live as if I was going to die tomorrow.

WYNTER: I hate that comment. That comment is ridiculous. If a person were going to die the next day, they would not pay their bills. People dying the next day, live very differently, than those that will live.

AUGGIE: I meant to imply, that the memories I make each day, should be so important, they "become the thoughts flashing before my eyes the seconds before I die."
WYNTER: Yeah, How did that work for you with a fourteen-ton bus resting on your chest?

SERENA: Life can't be defined by the last days of your life. It is a cumulative result of a lifetime of steps.

WYNTER: It's not the people that share your beliefs that make your faith and morals stronger.

AUGGIE: [*Proudly.*] Is it studying? I constantly studied lessons preparing my life, pushing others away that did not share my values.

SERENA: Wynter said it right. It's not the people sharing your beliefs, which make your faith and morals stronger. The people willing to "challenge" your belief system make your beliefs stronger.

WYNTER: We're not talking about political arguments. [*Pause.*] You know, when the other person demands debate, but within two seconds tells you you're a stupid idiot, because only stupid idiots don't share their view, and that is why everyone else are stupid idiots.

AUGGIE: Very few times bullies changed my mind in life. If anything, their viewpoint was lost, because now I had my walls up. Even if they were ultimately right, in my mind... they were now wrong.

WYNTER: Yes, but you were a popular speaker in the equality circles.

AUGGIE: No. I was a very controversial speaker, to those that preached equality.

WYNTER: You became controversial the moment you threw a fit on stage after one of the Equality Movement leaders demanded Republicans to leave the field, because they were not welcome at the rally.

AUGGIE: I was pissed. Not because he called them out as Republicans, but because he represented one of the highest positions in their organization, an organization that only uses the word equality, as long as it's defined with themselves being righteous.

WYNTER: I don't understand.

AUGGIE: To me, he was starting a dialogue by more or less telling them they are unworthy to hear our words.

SERENA: Because the speaker on stage demanded a choir of people praising his words.

AUGGIE: First, those people would not have attended unless they were sharing some of our beliefs.

SERENA: You need them on the field, so they can hear the message, to be inspired. You never inspire people by starting the dialogue by calling them stupid idiots.

AUGGIE: Nobody is equal until everyone is equal. Fighting for equality can't be something we do, by destroying others. We don't become better by belittling those around us, my Wynter taught me this in fourth grade. We need to reach out with open arms, to guide them though the journey. Their presence that day on the field told us they are willing to listen, to follow, and one-day help us lead.

WYNTER: But what if they are loud?

SERENA: Often the loudest person in the room, [*Points at Auggie.*] is the most insecure.

WYNTER: All day long, for at least a week you couldn't believe they chose you to be their first emcee.
SERENA: This is when you let me inspire you the most. I can remember you distinctly sitting in church struggling with God to give you a sign.

AUGGIE: I was! Any sign.

WYNTER: Yes. You were hoping God would speak to you in one of those
[*With deep voice imitating Jones.*] James Earl Jones voices. God was
listening.

AUGGIE: [*To Serena.*] Was it God that rescued my insecurities that day?

SERENA: [*Laughs. Starts to exit off STAGE RIGHT.*] You never get it Auggie.
All of your steps are not taken by God. God does not create your life. You
do.

AUGGIE: [*Turns to watch Serena walk off the stage.*] Was it you who put
that picture of Harvey Milk in my mind?

SERENA: [*Brushes her fingers in compliment off her opposite shoulder.*] It
worked, didn't it? In a flash, I was able to remind you, to change the
world; you don't need to look like a model. Simple people, with basic
messages change worlds Auggie.

AUGGIE: And the rest?

SERENA: [*Walking off the stage.*] The rest? You need to learn to focus
more energy on people helping you succeed. Stop wasting energy trying to
worry about …the rest. [*Serena exits.*]

AUGGIE: I like Serena. She scares the bajebies out of me. Much like my
grandfather. He never was mean to me, but something about him always
made me nervous.

WYNTER: Most grandfathers are that way. I believe because they are less
likely to be the silly, fun characters in your memories.

AUGGIE: My grandfather told me as a child, that if my sister and I didn't
shut up and go to sleep in their home on Christmas eve… he was going to
load up his shotgun and shoot Santa in the head.

WYNTER: [*Caught off guard. Bursts into laughter.*] Bet that shut you up
quickly.

AUGGIE: [Exiting Stage.] Very.

        [Both exit. Curtain opens.]

Act III BEST SAID DEAD
Scene Two

Time: 25.00

> *Curtain opens. The table with its balls and fake arm, and the ottoman are on top of the bed. On top of the pile is a large paper Mache animal approximately four to seven feet tall. You can use any tall animal (horse, giraffe, flamingo…).Victor is pacing around the bed looking at the pile. Oliver is sitting on the chair across the room.*

VICTOR: [*Already on a rant. Pacing back and forth around his bed.*] I know Serena did this to me. Wynter is not strong enough. Serena is messing with me. The bed is mine. I was promised the bed. This is unacceptable. What are going to do about it Oliver? I demand recourse.

Oliver: Recourse? Do you even know what that word is?

VICTOR: No, but I heard it on Judge Judy and the person won the case. You don't mess with Judy. I bet Serena wouldn't mess with Judy. [Victor instantly stops. You can tell he is trying to rationalize a flow chart.] Mercy, mercy, mercy!

OLIVER: What now Victor?

VICTOR: Serena is Judge Judy! You must be kidding me. Why didn't I get someone cool to mold. Everyone gets the fun ones except for me. Where is my Charlie Sheen? Where is my Mel Gibson? I demand someone fun! Oliver! At this point, I'll settle for Justin Beber!

OLIVER: There is a reason nobody invited you to utopia Victor. Everyone has a purpose here.

Victor: [*Starts taking the furniture down. Oliver remains seated.*] I don't understand. Why is this happening to me? It's not the first time everything in his mind got dumped onto my bed.

OLIVER: [Rising, speaking to Victor] His brain is not right. It has complications. You remember what happened when that movie, Beautiful Mind came out about schizophrenia. It took us weeks to clear your bed.

VICTOR: I totally forgot about that Russell Crowe movie. Oh my gosh. Yes, it was a big problem.

OLIVER: He quit a great job; became obsessed, perhaps his incredible life was a figment of his imagination, and in reality, he was sitting on the floor, coloring in a coloring book.

VICTOR: I remember as if it was yesterday. His best friend begging him to snap out of it, but his OCD had latched on full force.

OLIVER: You convincing him his best friend was placed in his brain as a figment of his imagination didn't help the situation.

VICTOR: It was funny. I thought it was funny. Looking back at it, I'm sure we will all laugh. Are you going to help me, take this pile down?

OLIVER: [sits back down in the chair] Guess I'm not ready to laugh yet.

VICTOR: Come on Ollie, you know the funniest moments in Auggie's life came from me. [*Grabs the paper mache animal.*] Remember when his friend made this for his old apartment?

OLIVER: [Rises, crosses to Victor] Will you stop calling me Ollie, and put down that papier-mâché (horse)!

VICTOR: [*Ignores Oliver, continues story.*] One late evening, Auggie was drunk, drunk, drunk. Came stumbling into the apartment complex and noticed the old trouble-making neighbor sitting across the courtyard before she could see him.

OLIVER: Yes. You made Auggie crawl into his apartment, leaving the lights off, opened the curtains, turned on a low light... [*Oliver cut off by a hysterical laugh. Victor imitates scene.*]

VICTOR: Auggie wiggled his fat belly across the floor, holding this (horse) for the old lady to see... [*Victor prances with the animal, like a Merry Go Round over his head, laughing louder.*] Auggie on the floor, on his back rolling across the carpeting, drunk as a skunk, laughing his butt off, while the old lady flipped out on her porch. Tell me that was not hysterically funny. It was funny, on that date, and it still is funny.

OLIVER: She called the police that night. Animal control came to Auggie's house twice that week.

VICTOR: [*Still laughing.*] Because she convinced the officers, Auggie had a (horse) hidden in his house. He had to move the paper art piece into his bedroom to avoid getting into trouble.

OLIVER: You made Auggie do it four times in one week. By the end of the month, the family placed her in a retirement home for her own safety.

VICTOR: [*Stops laughing suddenly.*] Okay, that part is not as funny. I didn't force Auggie to be me, he decided all on his own. [*Victor sits the animal on the dresser and finishes clearing the bed while Oliver speaks.*]

OLIVER: Auggie's daughter said it right years ago, "Auggie doesn't know how to be Auggie, without being The Infamous Auggie." He is too insecure to live without you, Victor.
VICTOR: You say it like that's a bad thing Ollie.

OLIVER: It is!

VICTOR: My feelings are hurt. [*Victor's bed is cleared except for the fake arm. He sits on the bed, looking at the sheets in disgust.*] I need new sheets!

WYNTER: [*Enters room.*] Get your own sheets!

VICTOR: [*Shocked by Wynter's transformation. Jumps off the bed. Runs to WYNTER.*] What have we here Madam Butterfly? Are you wearing mascara? How delightful!

WYNTER: Don't mess up my makeup!

VICTOR: [*To Oliver.*] Ollie, she smells of aqua net and [*Sniffs Wynter. Looks back to Oliver, surprised and impressed.*] ...and Chanel #5. Wow. [*Walking back to the bed.*] No wonder we can't afford new sheets.

OLIVER: You look beautiful Wynter.

WYNTER: [*Curtsy.*] Thank you. Serena spent the day, spoiling me. [*Picks up the animal and moves it to the table.*]

VICTOR: If Serena was with you, then who took this entire room, and sat it on top of my bed. [*Stands up and retrieves the animal back to the dresser.*] I happen to love this (horse). It reminds me of laughter.

WYNTER: It reminds me of every stupid dress up thing you ever inspired Auggie to do. That time you made him dress as an airplane pilot; a red long scarf hanging out the window.

VICTOR: [*Starts laughing again.*] He was the Red Baron! Made the trip fun. [*Hand gestures.*] A *propeller* mounted on the front of his AMC Pacer, with tiny foam *wings* on the side. Hilarious; classic Auggie moments.

OLIVER: I'm surprised he didn't get pulled over by the cops.

WYNTER: I'm surprised a passing truck didn't snag the scarf and yank his head off.

VICTOR: I made him fun. Even road trips were fun. What about this fake arm hanging out of his trunk for the Phoenix to Florida trip? [*Holds up the arm.*]

WYNTER: It was morbid. [Wynter grabs arm from Victor. Quickly Oliver grabs arm from WYNTER and places it on the dresser.]

OLIVER: The facial expressions on passing cars were funny. What made the joke witty, was the huge sign you placed above the arm that read, "Auggie Summers changed his facebook profile to SINGLE." [*Oliver laughs.*] Even I must admit, that was funny.

Victor: Precisely. Auggie's best stories are not of the wickedness I placed in him, but the confidence to laugh at himself. To appreciate the laughter of people.

WYNTER: I remember the woman at the gas station, telling Auggie her WYNTER was in the car panicking because the wind was blowing the arm, making it look like it was struggling to get out of the trunk.

VICTOR: What is it with all you old people missing the joke? I don't get it. If Jim Carrey does it, you give him twenty million dollars a movie, when I do it, it's insanity.

WYNTER: Precisely.

VICTOR: Please, if it wasn't for me, Auggie would still be a virgin. [*Exits STAGE RIGHT.*]

WYNTER: [*WYNTER walks over to the dresser opens the bottom drawer to pull out a set of bright white sheets. Sets them on the end of the bed.*] Let Poom waste his time searching for these sheets.

AUGGIE: [*Enters STAGE RIGHT. Still looking back at Victor.*] Are you coming back in here Victor? Hello. Hello Victor, Earth to Victor. Come in Victor. [*Auggie gives up. Enters room. Speaks to Oliver.*] Is it just me, Victor seems out of character this week?

OLIVER: Where have you been Auggie? You could easily get lost in here.

SERENA: [*Enters STAGE RIGHT dragging Victor by the hair.*] Auggie was with me. [*To Wynter, dragging Victor in by the hair.*] What did I say about feeding strays? [*To Victor, Pointing to the bed.*] Sit. Behave; else, I'm grabbing a rolled magazine to beat you into tomorrow.

VICTOR: [*Complaining.*] The hair, the hair. I don't have Wynter's budget to get my hair done.

OLIVER: [*To Serena.*] We love Wynter's new wardrobe. She looks stunning. I barely recognized her.

WYNTER: Does my outfit make me look fat?

VICTOR: No, I'm pretty sure your fat makes you look fat.

OLIVER, SERENA, and WYNTER: [*In harmony.*] Shut up Victor. [*Wynter walks over to sit on the floor near the stairs on LEFT APRON. Avoid eye contact with audience.*]

AUGGIE: [Holding his own gut] Yes, shut up Victor. This is why I had so many problems fighting for equality when I was alive. People making me feel unworthy to have a voice.

OLIVER: It's hard to fight for equality, when you look in a mirror and see less of a person looking back at you.

WYNTER: You always had your humor to buffer the preachiness of your message. I loved your humor, because it represented... me.

VICTOR: Yes, it was messy and made no sense.

SERENA: [*To Victor.*] Ignore him Wynter. No sense getting in a battle of wits with an unarmed man.

WYNTER: You always had a way of telling stories that mesmerized people. You would start re-telling an incident to a group of people; including the person in the story... even they were fascinated by your theatrics.

VICTOR: No, I'm sure many of them just wanted to hear how the story turned out, because it was a more clever story than reality.

SERENA: Victor, if you don't shut up, I'm going to sit on you.

VICTOR: Please do. I'm still paying child support to the last girl that thought I was safe enough to tempt.

OLIVER: [*To Victor.*] What am I going to do with you?

VICTOR: [*Flirtatious.*] I have a list. [Oliver glares at Victor.]

OLIVER: Temptation is everywhere Auggie. Like we said before, just because you are tempted doesn't require you to follow through. Freewill is not an invitation. Not everyone has the best intent.

AUGGIE: I know this. My WYNTER taught me to lock the car doors each time we went to church. She would say, "Not everyone is going to church today." It took me years to realize the sentence, was a warning for life.

VICTOR: Auggie, People with bad intentions go to church too.

SERENA: Yes, we call them sinners. It's what we do during redemption, which creates the people we become.

AUGGIE: It's bizarre, listening to all of you talking about me all the time. I know I made many mistakes, and for most of them, I paid a price.

SERENA: Not actually. Most people get away with their corrupt activity.

WYNTER: No. Actually most of the time people are caught because they made a mistake. Like the time, a decade ago, when computers confused me.

AUGGIE: Are you talking about me checking out porn on the computer?

VICTOR: No. I had you send some guy a bunch of naked pictures of yourself across the internet.

OLIVER: Serena threw a fit.

VICTOR: So I started rushing you to hit the send button.

SERENA: This is not a funny story.

WYNTER: I didn't know how to use a computer.

VICTOR: Seconds before you hit enter, I told you to send a copy to yourself. You began to type your email address, and your computer instantly offered the rest of your email address.

WYNTER: So I just had you click it, so Serena would stop screaming.

OLIVER: Victor had you instantly hit the enter button before Serena could stop you.

AUGGIE: I remember that day. It was the most embarrassing day of my life.

SERENA: I told you not to send it. You only have you to blame.

OLIVER: You hit that enter button at the same second I noticed the comma after your name.

AUGGIE: Yes, I had just sent the naked photos to every single person on my Christmas list.

SERENA: Serves you right.

VICTOR: I never heard you scream so loudly. A grown man in his underpants running through his home, screaming hysterically because he just sent six dirty photos to a hundred family and friend email accounts.

WYNTER: I couldn't stop screaming, and it made you start screaming.

VICTOR: Now that day was funny.

SERENA: Serves you right. I was just mad, cuz' Oliver gave you another Auggie moment by having you send an email, immediately warning people that the first message was a virus, so don't open it. Now to me, being stupid, is classic Auggie.

VICTOR: Yes WYNTER. When all else fails, read the directions.

OLIVER: I've been proud to be in your mind. See all of this Auggie? [*Points at audience.*] Row upon row of wonderful memories. You have managed to pack your life with splendid memories.

SERENA: If you fill your brain with good thoughts, you have no room for bad memories.

WYNTER: You were always so funny, often at your own expense. You made it too easy for Victor to tempt you.

VICTOR: I am the person your WYNTER warned you about.

SERENA: You would think with you as the oldest child, your parents would have been terrified to have more children.

OLIVER: You've lived a long life Auggie, you should be proud of the people that made your life so successful. Even when you were single, you proved you could cope, that single did not mean you were alone.

AUGGIE: I hated being single, unworthy to belong to anyone.

SERENA: Yes, but it destroyed many years of your life. The constant belief that other people make you whole. The more people you hooked up with to avoid loneliness, the more alone you felt.

OLIVER: Serena gave you the courage to lean on your friends, to stop being superficial, and to accept rejection. To learn to not be afraid of your age.

WYNTER: No matter what your dating profile age said, you were born the same year Hemingway died.

VICTOR: Yes, I am sure the Hemingway's no longer blame you.

AUGGIE: I left the world with so many people still angry with me.

WYNTER: Nobody leaves the world in perfect harmony.

SERENA: If that were the case, we would only have one religion, one belief, one political system, and everyone on the same page.

VICTOR: I demand change; well, as long as the change is to the stuff I support.

SERENA: Your friend came to the hospital once when you were sick. He brought you a large bouquet of colorful stuffed teddy bears, saying each bear represented a friend. He asked you which colored bear in the bundle represented you.

VICTOR: Sounds like that M&M candy test a psychiatrist gives, to see which colored candy the kid takes out of the bowl. [Mockingly.] *"Oh, your child selected a green M&M first. She will grow up having social anxiety, and perhaps an eating disorder."*

WYNTER: I forgot this teddy bear story. What color bear did you choose?

AUGGIE: I told my friend I wanted to be the red ribbon wrapped around the bears. I wanted to be the person that held my friends together.

WYNTER: Oh, such a pretty thing to say.

OLIVER: You were not a bad person Auggie; you just talk about your bad parts too much.

SERENA: I believe you spent too much time talking and writing about the bad parts of your past.

WYNTER: I agree. Even your daughter thought you spent too much time defining the bad parts of your life. I blame Victor.

SERENA: [*To Auggie.*] I blame you Auggie, and you are smart enough to stop blaming others. Believe in people around you. I must have told you this a hundred times. [*Starts to repeat her phrase but everyone on stage repeat it with her.*]

SERENA: [*Starts quote, after two words, the entire cast joins her in harmony.*] Push on…

SERENA, WYNTER, OLIVER, AUGGIE, VICTOR: [*In harmony.*] …Push Hard, and when you feel you don't have the energy to push, learn to believe your friends will carry you on.

OLIVER: Exactly. I believe it's guilt. Auggie felt guilty. When he was a bad person, his world rocked, he thought he had control. Think about it, never a night spent in jail. Lots of guilt knowing you can wiggle out of any situation.

VICTOR: Yes, not everyone gets the powers of Auggie Moments.

SERENA: Shut up with that Auggie Moments crap.

AUGGIE: What is an Auggie Moment? [Auggie gets defensive.] I'm not as stupid as I look!

WYNTER: Auggie Moment is a phrase Victor created each time you were
painted into a corner.

SERENA: Victor would change into this ridiculous club boy outfit in red,
and drive us all crazy singing and prancing across your brain to ABBA songs
until we helped you out of the situation.

VICTOR: It worked! If you don't like silly people, you will hate me.

WYNTER: Drove us crazy.

VICTOR: [*Mockingly.*] Short drive!

AUGGIE: I thought it was God answering my prayers.

SERENA: You don't ask God to help get you out of trouble for doing
something bad. Please, if it were up to Victor, the next time someone was
screaming at you, [Serena gets two inches from Oliver's face to mimic the
story.] you would remove the cellphone from your pocket, to hold six
inches from their face to snap a photo to place on facebook. Victor
doesn't teach you boundaries.

WYNTER: God did answer you. He said, "no." [Looking at Auggie.] Victor
wiggled you out of your problems.

VICTOR: Please, at Auggie's size, passing through doorways often took
wiggling. =.

WYNTER: Of course, [*Jumps to her feet and runs to Auggie's defense.*]
Auggie is a big man. [*Hugs Auggie's chest.*} How else could he hold such a
big heart? Anyway, Auggie... diets are for quitters.

VICTOR: [*Ignoring Wynter. Animated.*] Push piglet push. Pooh is caught in
the cave. He has been eating too much honey!

[*Wynter starts dragging the dresser off the STAGE LEFT.*]

SERENA: What are you doing? You're going to pull something.

OLIVER: Where are going with that dresser?

WYNTER: I don't know. Something tells me, it will look better over here.
[WYNTER pulls the dresser off the stage. Quickly runs back in screaming.] I
just saw a giant cockroach. It was so excited as it ran across the room... for
a moment, I thought it was a puppy!

AUGGIE: I always felt guilty. Towards the end of my life, I had little to offer my church, so I made my contributions up with my talent, because I ran low on cash.

SERENA: Most give more to a bartender than towards their religious beliefs. Look at all the times people tip fifteen percent to the waitress for an hour of her time, but freak out about the thought of tipping ten percent to their core beliefs.

OLIVER: It's one of the downfalls of social networking sites. Now you had nobody asking you for cash, few people offering, and 600 million people believing that hitting a LIKE button will save the world.

AUGGIE: [WYNTER and Victor start removing furniture.] Now, where you are going?

VICTOR: This table seems wrong. I need to move it.

OLIVER: Leave the table alone.

VICTOR: I can't leave it alone. It's wrong, all wrong. [*Victor walks the table off STAGE RIGHT. WYNTER re-enters the stage.*]

WYNTER: Here, let me help you. [*Wynter crosses the stage, passes Victor and grabs the ottoman.*] Auggie, when you were alive you wrote books by dictating the sentences to Oliver, correct?

AUGGIE: Yes.

WYNTER: That makes Oliver the writer.

AUGGIE: What does that make me?

WYNTER: The dictator.

OLIVER: Are you going to wax the floor? What are you two doing?

WYNTER: [*Re-enters the stage. WYNTER takes off the old sheets and pillows, leaving a single sheet covering the bed. Exits STAGE LEFT.*] Let me wash these linens. Auggie, did you ever make a list of everyone you let down?

AUGGIE: I don't need a list to know the people I let down. [*Wynter enters STAGE LEFT. Cuts to front of bed.*]

OLIVER: Do you know what they call such a list?

AUGGIE: No, not really.

OLIVER: A list of witnesses for the prosecution. [*Laughs. Notices WYNTER cleaning out from under the bed.*] Where are you going with all of this stuff? Why do I feel I'm losing control? This makes no sense. I didn't authorize any of these changes. Why are you cleaning? Why is everyone being so nice to each other? Where have you been Wynter? Something is wrong. [*WYNTER ignores everyone.*] Why must gay men be so confusing?

VICTOR: I am not gay. I just pretend to be gay, to hang out with all the cool people. [*Takes the chair on STAGE RIGHT and takes it off STAGE RIGHT. Serena sits on bed.*]

AUGGIE: Are you all right Wynter? [*Wynter walks past Auggie, heading towards the CENTER APRON. Auggie sits on bed.*]

OLIVER: Now where are you going Wynter? I told you specifically, yesterday, to stop harassing the rest of Auggie's imagination. [*Wynter walks past all of them, ignoring them. Wynter centers the APRON. Oliver throws his hands up in exasperation, and sits next to Serena and Auggie on the bed. The bed is all that remains on the stage.*]

WYNTER: [*Wynter pulls out a paper from her bra. On the bed, confused are Auggie, Serena, and Oliver. To the audience.*] I wrote you all a poem. You could imagine the difficulty in here of locating an ink pen that actually writes. [Wynter reads to Audience.]

Just believe what's in your heart, and in your soul that's kind,
Of happy thoughts and memories, buried in your mind.
Just believe in happiness, to dance your life, a waltz.
Just believe that people care, forget about their faults.

Build a world inside your soul, of goodness that you seek.
Forget about the ugliness, of the people that are weak.
Surround yourself with happy friends, unconditional love will flow.
For tomorrow's love and happiness, should be the only things you know.

I believe through primrose glass, that life can void all strife.
Focus in, on simple thoughts, to make your life, a life.
I will die a happy one, because I believe in you.
And hopefully inside your life, you believe, inside me too.

[Pause four seconds. A loud voice suddenly comes from on top the stage, startling everyone to their feet. WYNTER runs back to the end of the bed. Victor runs back into the room. Everyone is looking up.]

DOCTOR: Auggie, can you hear me Auggie? Auggie.

WYNTER: Oh my, where is that man's voice coming from?

OLIVER: I don't know. Everything is so out of control.

AUGGIE: Is it God?

SERENA: I don't believe God would have to ask if you can hear him or not. It's not like you're alive to ignore him.

VICTOR: *[Picks up any stray balls or clutter on the floor.]* I'm out of here. Justin Bieber here I come! *[Exits STAGE LEFT.]*

DOCTOR: Auggie. Auggie.

WYNTER: *[Runs down steps on STAGE LEFT.]* I saw this on Montel Williams

SERENA: It's not Montel Williams.

OLIVER: It's not God.

AUGGIE: Who is it Wynter?

SERENA: *[Check for any items left under the bed.]* I had better go pack. *[Serena exits STAGE RIGHT.]*

AUGGIE: This is confusing.

OLIVER: WYNTER?

WYNTER: It's a séance. I saw it on Montel. Someone from the living world is trying to get his spirit's attention. *[Wynter starts acting excitedly, running through the audience.]* What am I supposed to do? Do I get to blow out a candle, make a table float in the air?

OLIVER: What do you mean, like in the movie Ghost?

WYNTER: I want to play. Can I bring a penny up the wall? Please Oliver, can I freak out Whoopi Goldberg? *[Runs back up on stage. Pushes the bed out STAGE RIGHT. The stage is now empty.]*

AUGGIE: Is it a new person coming to join us?

WYNTER: [*Runs back on stage from STAGE RIGHT with a sheet half over her head.*] Should I put the sheet over my head?

> [*Suddenly the lights go out. In the darkness, the gurney is moved to CENTER STAGE, with Victor still hiding underneath the bed. Make sure the sheet is over Auggie, with the pillow under his head. Oliver and Wynter are off stage. The doctor, in a white coat, moves next to the bed, UPSTAGE near Auggie's head. Lights remain off.]*

DOCTOR: Auggie, [*Keeps repeating the name Auggie in the darkness, until stage is set. The next sentence is the key words to turn on only a spotlight to follow the doctor next to Auggie's head.*] Are you all right Auggie?

AUGGIE: [*Looking puzzled around the room.*] Where... Where am I?

DOCTOR: Bassett Memorial Hospital.

AUGGIE: I don't understand. Where is Oliver?
DOCTOR: Is that your boyfriend?

AUGGIE: Where's Wynter?

DOCTOR: Your daughter called your mom an hour ago.

AUGGIE: My daughter is in ...here?

DOCTOR: Yes, she's down in the cafeteria getting a coffee. We called her when the ambulance brought you in. We thought we had lost you. You died, you know.

AUGGIE: I do know actually.

DOCTOR: [*Puzzled by Auggie's response.*] Well, ...okay, I guess. I've read about people dying, and hovering above their bodies.

AUGGIE: How long was I dead? Weeks?

DOCTOR: [*Laughs.*] Hardly, they just brought you in here a few hours ago Sport. Two minutes dead tops; loss of blood from your head wound. You passed out in the bus.

AUGGIE: Two minutes?

DOCTOR: Did your life flash before your eyes?

AUGGIE: No, doctor. Not at all.

DOCTOR: Your daughter will be up here in a few minutes Mr. Summers.
[*Doctor starts to leave. Remembers something, turns to Auggie.*] You
know Sport. We've met before.

AUGGIE: We have? Where?

DOCTOR: I tried picking you up at Charlie's. Bought you a beer. You more
or less ignored me. Too bad. [*Leaves.*] I used to think you were attractive.

AUGGIE: [*Fixing his hair. Realizes his head has a large Band-Aid on it.*]
Ouch! Now you tell me. [*Pause. Nods.*] Voices in my head. Figures.
Where are they when I need to pick up a doctor?

VICTOR: [*Pops up the sheet on the bed, showing his face, from under the
bed. Shouts.*] Go for it Auggie, go for it!

SERENA, OLIVER, and WYNTER: [*In unison.*] Shut up Victor!

Lights turn off. End of Act III
End of Play.

We asked each person buying a ticket to help those struggling to find food,
by bringing a can of food for the food pantry charity. People donated bags.

TAMPA CAST (Left to Right). Jeremy McDonald (Auggie), Playwrights Todd Kachinski-Kottmeier and Steve Hammond (Oliver), Jeffrey T. Casey (Serena), Sharon Kachinski (Play is dedicated to her), Justin Duncan (Victor), Tea Sotelo (Wynter), and George Summers (Both God and Emergency Room Doctor).

The volunteers from ticket collectors, ushers, and hosts

"It's what you do during redemption that determines your character."

"Run through life for there is plenty of time to rest at the end."

Tea Soleto takes stage as the first Wynter to perform as Wvnter.

"Drunk, Drunk, Drunk…"

Lili Pearls shows the love of a coast.

Playwright's Sharon Kachinski, is joined by Todd's daughter Cheryl and her husband

The cast joins Melissa Green on Tampa's Opening Night.

ISBN-13:
978-1725086685

ISBN-10:
1725086689
Artwork of both scripts by Rick C. Moore

Third Edition
Copyright © 2012, 2014, and 2018 Todd Kachinski

Both plays, "Best Said Dead" or "Following Wynter" cannot be performed "in full" or "in parts without prior written consent of Todd Kachinski Kottmeier

DRAG411's Ten Black Books

Book 1:	**DRAG411's "DRAG Bully, A Survivor's Guide"**
	Copyright © 2015 and 2018
Book 2:	**DRAG411's "Original DRAG Handbook"**
	Copyright © 2010, 2011, 2012, 2014, and 2018
Book 3:	**DRAG411's "Crown Me! Winning Pageants"**
	Copyright © 2013, 2014, and 2018
Book 4:	**DRAG411's "DRAG King Guide"**
	Copyright © 2014 and 2018
Book 5:	**DRAG411's "DRAG Stories"**
	Copyright © 2011, 2014, and 2018
Book 6:	**DRAG411's "DRAG WYNTER, DRAG Father"**
	Copyright © 2012, 2014, and 2018
Book 7:	**DRAG411's "Spotlight Today"**
	Copyright © 2012 and 2018
Book 8:	**DRAG411's "DRAG Queen Guide"**
	Copyright © 2014 and 2018
Book 9:	Two Comedy Scripts:
	DRAG411's "Best Said Dead"
	Copyright © 2011, 2014, and 2018
	"Following Wynter"
	Copyright © 2012, 2014, and 2018
Book 10:	**DRAG411's "DRAG World"**
	Copyright © 2012 and 2018

From the best-selling author of "CommUnity of Transition,"
"Two Days Past Dead," The Novel and the sequel,
"Turn Around Bright Eyes, the DRAG Queen Killer,"
"Joey Brooks, The Show Must Go On," and
"Waiting On God."

Following Wynter

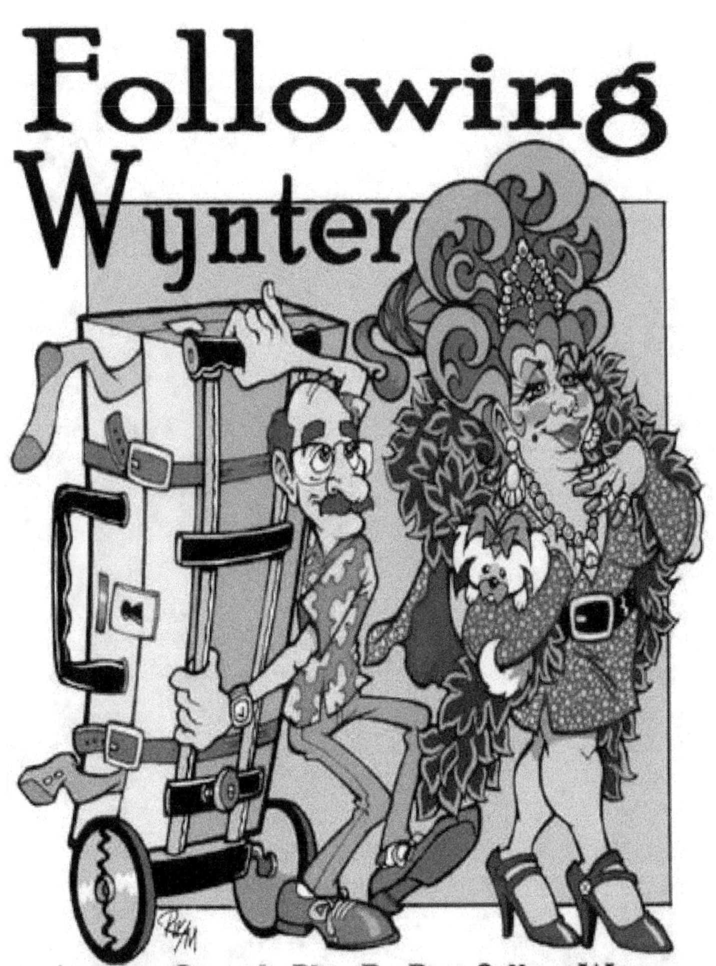

Another Comedy Play By Best Selling Writer
Todd Kachinski Kottmeier with Steve Hammond

Cast
[In order of Appearance]

All roles can be male, female, neither, or both!

Chulo Sotelo Meraz Fernandez de Santiago/Wynter Storm
Hispanic male.

Jonathon Powers/Serena Silvers
Distinguished retired drag queen; lives transgendered as a female.

Ethan Evans
A mousey quiet bookkeeper.

Daniel Flowers
An attractive community theater actor (or actress). Very flamboyant off stage. Uses theater to become a different person. Daniel has been in the closet his entire life.

Stage

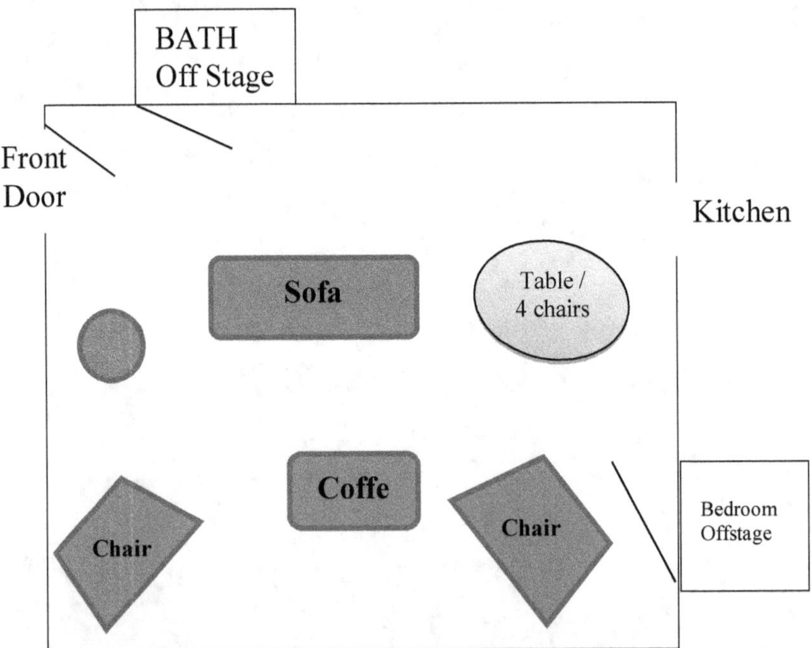

Act I Following Wynter
Scene One
Time: 3:00

Narrator: [Enters living room from kitchen, eating a bowl of spaghetti, looking around the room. Suddenly (s)he notices the audience.] Oh dear, I didn't see you sitting there. [Sits the bowl and spoon on the dining room table. Approaches center apron.] Have you been here the entire time? [Center apron.] Good evening, [Reaches out to shake, but realizes there is spaghetti sauce on his/her hand. Narrator withdraws hand, and wipes it on his/her pants.] Spaghetti sauce, sorry. You see, Ethan makes the most incredible spaghetti. I've been his neighbor for the past twelve years. [Pause. Looks around auditorium.]

I hope you are not going to tell on me for sneaking in his back door to eat. It's not like I break in every day. Just a few times a week. Simple stuff. A snack. Toilet Paper. A dab of toothpaste. You know, the things you forget to pick up from Whole Foods after work. [Pause. Pointing out the room to the audience.] Look at this place. No television. Everything in its place, nothing out of order. Nothing to steal, not a place I would ever hang out on my own. Don't get me wrong, I love going out for a cocktail with Ethan, as long as it's at Applebee's. I'm not going to do that gay bar stuff. I think he calls his bar the front door here's my back door, or something along those lines.

[Whispers.] He's one of those ...gays. [Clarifying, in regular voice.] Don't get me wrong, I have nothing against [Using fingers to denote words.] "the gays," obviously... one of my best friends is gay. Actually, I don't think he really fits into the gay stereotype. He's not a dashing dresser, I can take the stuff from his home because he shops in bulk at Costco. Ethan is very practical, extremely conservative; I met his new husband, went to their wedding. Chulo's a very tough man. I could see him dating my daughter. A man's man! Not those fancy gay types you see on television or shopping at Trader Joes. [Turns to exit to kitchen.] We live in a very close knit cul-de-sac, everyone knows everyone's business. I'm pretty confident... [Pause. Exiting.] I'm the only person that knows Ethan is one of those [drawn out.] homosexuals. [Shrugs. Exits.]

Act I Following Wynter
Scene Two
Time: 30:00

> *Curtains are already open to an empty stage. You hear screaming from off stage. Chulo runs from the front door with his arms in the air. He is holding an open box he is moving into the house. He runs into the living room, around the kitchen table, and the dining room chairs, around the couch, tossing the box in the air, and disappears into the kitchen. The whole time he is screaming for no apparent reasons. This is his entrance. You can hear him rustling under the sink and through pots and pans from the kitchen area. Place a hairspray and perfume used from the box upright behind the couch, so they are not part of the contents lost as they hit the floor from the first packing box.*

CHULO:
[*Off stage in kitchen*] Are you kidding me Serena, are you kidding me? [*Chulo enters. Rushes to contents he dumped on the floor from the box.*] What man does not have a can of Raid under the sink? This will do... [*Chulo picks up spray bottle and prepares to exit front door just as Serena enters.*]

SERENA:
[*Enters carrying a four-foot wig that she can barely balance in her hands. She places it on the side table next to couch STAGE RIGHT, knocking a lamp and a few other well-placed objects from the table.*] Where are you going with that bottle of perfume?

CHULO:
[*Still panicked.*] To kill those hornets once and for all. I'm not moving all my stuff into my new home with a hornet's nest on the porch!

SERENA:
With perfume Wynter? [*Serena looks down at the clutter all over the floor, nods head in disbelief. Bends over, pulls up a large can. Grabs the perfume from Chulo.*] At least use Aqua Net. [*Chulo exits back out front door; holding can of Aqua Net.*] Don't get me wrong Chulo, I adore your new husband. I never thought I would live to see the day that two men could walk down the aisle to marry each other legally.

CHULO:
[*Enters front door wiping sweat.*] The battle is far from over Serena. Between some states writing rules to block it and other parts of the country creating registries instead of marriages... well let's just say Ethan and I are fortunate to live in Boston.

SERENA:
I believe the registries are a good compromise. It's another stone in the path.

CHULO:
It's a tiny stone to shut us up for now.

SERENA:
I totally disagree with you. We live in a country where the federal government made gay marriage an option not available at this time. It's not a right [Pause] if you have to vote on it. These registries are created by our allies to prove to us they are on our side.

CHULO:
I don't know. To me it's like if Lincoln had said, we will free the slaves but only on paper, just as long as they don't actually believe they can exercise the right to be free. Either you are free or you are not free.

SERENA:
If we win one small town, one little village, soon it becomes a county. County by county signing on, eventually wins a state. It does not take a majority of states to change laws. It takes the will of the few, to pressure those in Washington to change legislation.

CHULO:
It seems like a long process.

SERENA:
[Walks to Chulo to show Chulo his ring.] Time is flying fast Chulo, and today you are representing.

CHULO:
[Seems puzzled.] I don't understand. What do Ethan and my ring represent?

SERENA:
Millions of gays and lesbians fighting a battle to share the same moment the two of you created last week. Your ring defines a nation of ideas and promise of what the "best of us can bring to the world." Your ring is a symbol of hundreds of thousands of people killed because of their orientation, and it honors the millions throughout history that never believed this day would become reality.

CHULO:
[*Nervously laughs, trying to lighten the moment.*] Damn girl, I hope they're going to help pay this ring off from JCPenny's. [*Laughs. Chulo picks up the tossed box from behind the couch to move into the bedroom.*] I don't know where I'm going to place all these boxes. Living with my WYNTER in Key West made hiding my clutter from Ethan so much easier. [*Exits to bedroom.*]

SERENA:
Considering your WYNTER never let Ethan into the back of the house when he was on vacation, he never realized how much clutter you created. [*Serena crosses to the huge wig sitting on the end table.*] Chulo, for the life of me, I don't know how you hid the fact from Ethan you are the fabulous Wynter Storm. I promise honey… [*Serena tries to pick up the wig but gives up and sets it back down.*] The secret is out in full force when he walks in that door after work.

CHULO:
[*Enters living room.*] Yes, but remember, For better or worse!

SERENA:
[*Laughs.*] Yes, dear, but the sentence also ends with "til death do us part.' [*They both laugh. Chulo's cell phone rings some obnoxious Spanish ringtone.*]

CHULO:
[*Looks at phone. Grins. Into cell phone.*] Pookie!

SERENA:
[*Exiting apartment to get the duffle bags, massive boxes, and dresses that will cover every single piece of furniture on the entire stage while they both speak.*] My dog when I was six was named Pookie. Since when did pet names for our spouse actually become pet names? [*Exits front door.*]

CHULO:
[*Brushing off Serena's comment. Speaking to Ethan on phone.*] It's Serena. She's been reading me from the second our U-Haul left my mom's in Key West until now. Now she's complaining about my new home. [*Pause.*] Nothing honey, just Serena whining about the hornet's nest on the porch. She's throwing a hissy because you don't have any Raid. [*Pause.*] Oh, it's in the laundry room. [*Pause.*] I told her you had some, [*Serena begins to enter,*] but you know Serena, always making drama out of nothing.

> Serena enters carrying six massive duffle bags, placing them across the couch, exhausted. She overhears the last part of Chulo's sentence.

SERENA:
I'm not being a drama queen about hauling your stuff in the house while you entertain on the phone. [*Serena opens up one of the duffle bags. She pulls out an empty plastic gallon milk jug and a closed pizza box.*] Are you kidding me? [*Shows Chulo.*] You rented a U-Haul to carry trash 1,663 miles up I-95?

CHULO:
[*To Serena.*] I had a wardrobe idea in my head.

SERENA:
You have a screw loose in your head Wynter. They sell pizza and milk in Boston. [*Opens the pizza box and a half pizza falls to the floor with a loud, hard thud upstage behind the chair on STAGE RIGHT. Screams.*] Wynter!

CHULO:
[*Turns his back on Serena. Serena exits stage to outside.*] Nothing honey. I'm so happy to be here officially. I never in a million years thought I would retire to Boston from Key West. [*Pause.*] No, no, no. I'm happy. The chance of you starting your bookkeeping practice from scratch in Florida is impractical. [*Walks over to the four-foot wig. Runs his hands through the top of the wig's hair.*] I have some ideas for part time income. You did say, you wouldn't mind if I worked for a few hundred dollars a week, right? [*Pause.*] Yes, baby. You did say, you would love me, even if I got a job as a dishwasher. [*In walks Serena holding a dozen dresses on hangers in each hand. Chulo grabs one of the dresses and places it in front of her, as if trying it on. Pause. Repeats very strategically, as if to remind Ethan again.*] Yes, I know… you will love me even if I get a job as a dishwasher.

SERENA:
[*Places each set of dresses on a different chair in the living room.*] It was bad enough you forced me to drive the entire trip because you couldn't read a map, but I refuse, REFUSE, to unload the trailer while you stare at me.

CHULO:
[*To Ethan.*] I'll talk to you when you get home in a few minutes. Can you pick up some Dr. Pepper please? [*Pause.*] No, I gave up smoking…

SERENA:
Oh good grief, you did not.

CHULO:
[*To Ethan.*] Okay, pick up a pack, it will last me a week. Love you Pookie bear. [*Making loud kissing noise. Serena squirms. Chulo turns off phone. Tosses it on couch.*] I can't read a map! [*Exits to outside, followed by Serena.*]

SERENA:
We didn't even have a damn map. It was one road, I-95. It was I-95 when we left and two days later, it was still I-95. Getting off an exit to buy your Fudge Rounds and Skittles don't count as a shift in the driving route. [*Offstage you hear Chulo mocking Serena.*]

CHULO:
Blah, blah, blah, blah. Blah, Blah, blah, Wynter, blah, Wynter, blah, blah.

> *Onstage we hear Chulo's phone starting to ring. Long pause to allow the obnoxious music ring to continue. In comes Chulo, almost running forward with the box the size of a Maytag washer. Serena is carrying the other side walking backwards, screaming at Chulo to slow down before dropping the box. Across the side panel in large black letters read, "Shoes 1 of 3."*

SERENA:
Slow down Speedy Gonzalez, before you knock me on my butt. [*They walk the box to the kitchen table.*]

CHULO:
It's my mom. I was supposed to call her to tell her I made it to Boston alive with you driving.

SERENA:
The day is still young; the jury is out.

> *Sit box on table. Serena rolls her eyes as she exits stage to outside. Chulo is tearing the stuff from the couch trying to locate his phone. By the time he finds it, the duffle bags and the couch cushions are all over the floor. The phone is the only item left on the couch. The ringing stopped. Chulo stares at the phone, screaming at it.*

CHULO:
Really? Really? You saw me looking for you and you still sent my mom to voicemail. [*Mutters.*] This wouldn't have happened if I had AT & T. [*Hits redial. Pause. Scrunches face. To person on cell.*] Say what? [*Sits on STAGE RIGHT side of the couch.Chulo looks at dial. Realizes the person calling was not his WYNTER.*] Oh mercy, I thought I was hitting the redial to talk to my WYNTER. [*Pause. Becomes very polite.*] Yes Mr. Summers, I'm in Boston now. [*Pause.*] I got married here last week, flew home to move up. [*Pause.*] Oh, I see… you read it on facebook. [*Pause.*] No, sir. Yes, sir. No sir. Yes, sir. No, sir, Yes, sir. [*Rolls eyes.*] I understand, but I'll still be competing for the Miss Drag World Florida Classic Pageant in two weeks. [*Matter-of-factly.*] I'm expecting to win you know. [*Pause.*] I need to represent Florida at Nationals in December. [*Pause.*] No, I didn't know that my backup dancer was arrested yesterday, I was on the road. [*Sits on couch. Very sad.*] I'll still be there, with a new dancer. Serena Silver is sitting here with me. She won Drag World Classic National two years ago. [*Pause.*] Serena will help me find a new dancer in Boston. [*Now nervously.*] Yes, I know you know who Serena is sir; I wasn't name dropping. Yes sir, I'll make it right. You can count on us. I'll be there. [*Pause.*] I'm expected to win this year you know. [*Serena enters with two more boxes. She hears Chulo once again repeat. Notices Chulo upset.*] I'm expected to win. [*Chulo is almost in tears.*]

SERENA:
[*Piles boxes on top of dining room table.*] Tell me Wynter, what's wrong? Is your WYNTER okay? [*Serena starts to fan herself.*] Oh dear lord, I can't take it, if you tell me something happened to WYNTER Sotelo Meraz Fernandez de Santiago.

CHULO:
It's just as bad.

SERENA:
Chulo, you know you can count on me, we can work our way through anything? Tell me, what happened.

CHULO:
[*Breaks down.*] Hector can't dance for me, he's in jail for indecent exposure. Got drunk and went to the Duval Street Denny's and exposed himself by peeing on their wall.

SERENA:
Wynter! Hector peeing outside on the wall of Denny's is not the same thing as your WYNTER dying.

CHULO:
He was in the dining room.

SERENA:
What?

CHULO:
Standing on the table near the front door!

SERENA:
What?

CHULO:
Wearing a white halter-top!

SERENA:
What? Past Labor Day? Does he have no shame? [*Chulo's cell phone starts ringing again. Serena stands.*] I need one of those phones so I can stop constantly working. [*Chulo looks at screen and answers phone.*]

CHULO:
Hi Mom.

SERENA:
[*Exiting back outside.*] Tell your mom that someone unable to dance for you is just as upsetting as her dying. I'm pretty sure she'll be impressed with her value in your life. [*Exits.*]

CHULO:
[*To WYNTER.*] Nothing, just Serena sending her love. [*Pause.*] About thirty hours of driving with breaks. I was so nervous having that trailer going through the mountains. Mom, you accidently packed my trash bag into one of the duffle bags? [*Pause.*] We're unloading the car right now before Ethan gets home from work. I was hoping to enjoy our first night together, but one of his clients came out of the closet last week and Ethan is trying to help him through his family rejecting him. [*Chulo notices the pizza sitting on the floor, hidden from the audience. He reaches down and picks it up.*] I don't understand the details, but I guess the man is coming over tonight… [*Smells pizza.*] for dinner, [*Bites into pizza.*] for pizza. [*Place a clean half pizza hidden from the audience behind chair. Do not eat the actual pizza off the floor. Chulo shrugs his shoulder, mimicking the pizza is not bad.*] No, I'm not cooking, I've been driving for two days. [*Chulo stands. Noticeably sits pizza onto the bare couch near STAGE RIGHT. Serena enters with three more boxes. Walks to couch, unable to see over the boxes. Serena sits the boxes on top of the pizza. Chulo does not notice, as he's attempting to stand on the coffee table. To Serena.*] Hey Serena, a stage!

SERENA:
[*Upset.*] Get off the furniture. What are you twelve years old? Get off the phone. Do you expect me to do all your work while you prance around here like it's a day spa. This is the reason I'm staying at the Marriott. I can't live with your constant messes, it's gross.

CHULO:
[*Rolls eyes. To WYNTER, as he gets off the table.*] Sorry mom, I have to let you go. As you can tell, Serena doesn't like me talking to you when she demands attention. [*Chulo makes it a point to show Serena she is turning off the telephone.*]

SERENA:
I don't get it. You rarely work, you're always goofing off, you find an excuse to avoid any household chore, and [*Showing Chulo the now cluttered house.*] ...you are the messiest person on earth, and you get pissed at the only people that will help you, because [*Phonetically sounding out the words.*] "God forbid someone would ask you to help them, help you," and even then you find a way to pass yourself off as the victim.

CHULO:
Why must everything be so dramatic, so over the top with you? I was being silly, trying to have fun after a long trip. I will get to everything.

SERENA:
I've known you for three decades wench. The only thing you know how to get to... is a box from Dunkin Donuts.

CHULO:
At least I don't look like a drug addict, wasting away. I used to wonder if you were anorexic in high school.

SERENA:
I remember a time when the entire country thought people were gay if they were lean.

CHULO:
Scrawny, whimpy.

SERENA:
Lean, as in thin.

CHULO:
Please you couldn't make me look thin, even if you tossed me into a wood chipper.

SERENA:
An experiment I'm willing to try if you don't get outside. I need your help clearing out this rental truck, so I can get it off my charge card. [Pause] Everyone knows I'm gay, no matter what size I am. People look at my incredible clothes and they know I must be gay. I'm like a rainbow sticker Wynter. [Exit back outside.]

CHULO:
Please, you don't need incredible clothes to look gay Serena. You are like placing a rainbow sticker on a man's Mazda Miata... redundant. [Exits yelling.] Ethan! Honey. [You now see Ethan at the door trying to pick up Chulo to carry him through the door.] Oh dear.

ETHAN:
[Struggling to no avail.] It seemed so much simpler in my imagination.

CHULO:
Even I don't have that large of an imagination. [Serena comes from behind and pushes them both through the door. Ethan has his back to the rest of the room.]

SERENA:
I'm going to punch the next person that gives him an excuse to not work. We need to get the truck unpacked so I can get it returned by eight.

CHULO:
[Leans over and kisses Ethan.] Thank you for the thought Pookie. It's not like I'm a blushing bride. [Chulo follows Serena back out the front door.]

ETHAN:
Well I hope not, you would look scary in a [Turns to face living room.] ...dress. [Ethan looks terrified as he walks towards the dining room table.] What has happened to my house? [In walks Serena backwards carrying another huge box. This box has the words "WIGS, Brown/Red" scribbled in dark marker across the side. Daniel is helping Serena carry this box. Serena almost knocks over Ethan.]

SERENA:
Grand Central! [*Ethan ignores the push. He is visibly shaken by the disaster across his apartment. Serena looking at Daniel.*] Look what I found in your front yard. A stray. Can I keep him? [*Daniel is staring slowly around the room.*]

DANIEL:
[*Suddenly screams to Ethan.*] Oh my God, you've been robbed!

ETHAN:
[*To Serena.*] Serena, what happened to my house? [*Serena points to the outside door, towards Chulo. Ethan realizes the cat is missing and the front door is open. He begins to run to door.*] Willow! Willow? Have you had this door open all this time?

SERENA:
[*Lies with a very guilty expression.*] If this is where I'm supposed to say, No... then definitely... absolutely... "No the door was not left open." [*Serena and Daniel glance around for the cat. Ethan closes door. Daniel is downstage center in front of the back of chair.*]

ETHAN:
I've had Willow for almost fifteen years. I would be crushed if something happened to my Willow.

DANIEL:
Do you want me to look outside?

SERENA:
Don't be silly, we haven't even looked inside yet. [*Suddenly the front door swings open. Chulo enters carrying a body suit with built in breasts and padded buttocks.*]

CHULO:
Who shut the door? I can't carry stuff and turn the door knob at the same time.

ETHAN:
I shut the door Papi. I could not handle Willow being run over in traffic.

CHULO:
[*Glances slowly left. Slowly right, scrunching face.*] Oops. Hmmm, would it help... if I told you... we locked Willow in the bedroom so she would not get hurt?

ETHAN:

[*Looks visibly relieved as he hugs Chulo, turns and walks over and shuts front door.*] Oh, thank you Papi. I love you so much. [*Turns. Chulo looks at Serena revealing to Serena her betrayal of manipulating the words with a shrug and twist of the face. Chulo raises his two fingers to his eyes than to the bedroom, indicating for Serena to look in the bedroom for the cat. Serena exits to bedroom to look for Willow. Chulo walks to CENTER STAGE in front of the chair to introduce himself to Daniel.*]

CHULO:

[*To Daniel.*] You must be Daniel. [*Reaches out to shake hands. Ethan exits to kitchen. Daniel lightly shakes hand. Chulo looks at his own hand. Chulo refuses to let go of Daniel's hand.*] If that is how you shake a hand as a man, then I'm surprised people don't confuse you for a school girl. Give me your hand. Let me show you how a man shakes a hand. [*Daniel tries to pull his hand away, but Chulo pulls it back hard to show him how to shake like a man.*]

DANIEL:

[*Visibly in pain. Let's out an uncomfortable groan, catching Chulo off guard.*] Ouch.

[*As Chulo pulls back, he notices the white bandage on Daniel's wrist. Nothing is said during this exchange. All the interaction of Chulo's concern and Daniel's regret are done with eye contact. Chulo forces Daniel's hand towards him. Chulo using his free hand peels back Daniel's sleeve to reveal soiled bandages around his wrist. Chulo pauses; face very solemn, Daniel bows his head in shame. He looks like he will cry. Chulo uses both hands to gently set Daniel's wrist to his left side, Daniel does not look up. Chulo reaches down with his left hand and raises Daniel's right hand. Chulo slowly opens the sleeve on Daniel's right arm to reveal a white bandage around the wrist. Once again, Chulo uses both hands to set Daniel's arm back to his side. Chulo reaches in without a word and hugs him. Daniel's head is behind Chulo's. You can tell Chulo is emotionally impacted by this revelation. Pause. Ethan enters from KITCHEN. He is holding a bottle of beer.*]

ETHAN:

[*Jokingly.*] Not here five minutes and already Daniel is trying to sleep with my man. [*Laughs. Daniel and Chulo laugh. Chulo releases Daniel hands. Daniel looks for a place to sit. Walks over to edge of living room table and sits on the edge facing CENTER STAGE.*]

CHULO:
[*Walks to the clothes on the RIGHT STAGE chair. He picks them up and places them on the opposite chair on CENTER STAGE. Screaming to Serena.*] Serena, I know where everything is in that nightstand, sweetie!

ETHAN:
Oh mercy. [*Looks around the room. Ethan starts moving the items from the couch to the floor.*] Daniel, you can put Serena's dresses on the backs of the kitchen chairs. I'm shocked Serena brought so many dresses considering she's only here for two weeks. [*Picks up a dress that is extremely too large to ever be Serena's.*] Where did all of this come from, and where are we going to put it all? My house is only 912 square feet honey. Correction; **our** house is only 912 square feet.

DANIEL:
[*Moves dresses to dining room table chair down stage. Sits in CENTER STAGE chair.*] Square? I thought your house with the garage is shaped as an "L" It's not square.

CHULO:
[*Laughs.*] I miss being naive. I haven't been innocent since my family came over on a raft from Cuba.

ETHAN:
Have to thank Jimmy Carter for that.

DANIEL:
You moved all the way from Cuba to Florida?

SERENA:
Honey, Cuba is only ninety miles from Florida.

DANIEL:
Hold on... by boat or plane?

ETHAN:
What? Are you kidding me? [*Slowly Ethan removes the last box from the couch. He reaches down to peel the remaining pizza smashed into couch.*] I just got this couch.

CHULO:
[*Laughs, jumps up. Runs over to grab the pizza and take it the KITCHEN.*] Sorry, sorry, sorry. I promise; I'm planning to clean it up any minute now.

SERENA:
[*Enters from bedroom. Walking over to help Ethan place the cushions back on the couch.*] If I only had a bra for every time I heard that comment. [*Leans over to kiss the side of Ethan's head.*] Good afternoon Ethan, glad to see you again. [*Serena glances back at the KITCHEN.*] Are you sure you're ready for this... this [*Pause.*] Tasmanian devil.

ETHAN:
I know it's hard to move into a new place, I just never realized it would create such a mess.

DANIEL:
I can help clean up. I can't dance tonight.

SERENA:
[*Reaches over to shake Daniel's hand*.] Where are my manners. I'm Serena Silver, but you can call me- [*Cut off by Chulo entering the room.*]

CHULO:
Call her Wynter, I dare you!

SERENA:
[*Ignoring Chulo.*] Call me Serena. [*Daniel brushes past the handshake and rushes over to Serena to give a tight hug.*] Oh my, aren't we the mushy one. Don't hug me too hard, not everything in here is strapped down securely. [*Daniel keeps hugging. Serena looks uncomfortable. Serena peels Daniel off, as if he is a dirty diaper.*] Okay, okay, I get it... you don't do the handshake deal. [*Both take their seats. Ethan is still standing. Chulo approaches him to hug him.*]

CHULO:
I'm so glad you answered my dating profile when you were on vacation. I never thought there would be a day I would meet such a wonderful man. [*Hugs Ethan. Daniel is staring at Serena.*] I promise, I'm planning on putting all of this away by- [*Interrupted.*]

SERENA:
Next Christmas.

CHULO:
No, 4 pm

SERENA:
OK, next Christmas Eve.

ETHAN:
[*Kisses her before they both take their seats on STAGE RIGHT, Ethan back on the couch, Chulo on chair. Ethan is looking at the four-foot wig on the side table, next to the couch.*] I guess we can put some of Serena's props and stuff in the garage.

SERENA:
Props? I didn't bring any props.

ETHAN:
Dresses.

SERENA:
To move? Only Lady Gaga would wear a dress for moving.

CHULO:
[*Changing conversation.*] So Daniel, you're a dancer?

DANIEL:
Yes, sir?

SERENA:
A dancer or a stripper?

DANIEL:
I do Community Theater; [*Proudly*] we just finished a production of No, No Nanette. Actual singing and dancing; nothing like a stripper at a bar unable to dance, or a drag queen barely able to lip synch.

SERENA:
Don't get fresh with me.

ETHAN:
You're not a drag queen.

DANIEL:
She has an Adam's apple.

SERENA:
Of course I have a damn Adam's apple; most men do. I look dazzling in women's clothes. I'm not pretending to be a woman. I believe I look incredible in rabbit fur. That does not make me Bugs Bunny.

ETHAN:
I'm not being rude, all of this is complicated. I don't go to show bars. I go to this small neighborhood beer bar down the street called "Red Door Blue Door."

CHULO:
You've watched a drag queen perform. Many of them are men during the day, and just like Serena, they turn into glamorous movie stars at night.

SERENA:
Glamorous, dazzling…

DANIEL:
So you do drag?

SERENA:
That's what men that dress as girls call it when they put on a face; I just don't perform anymore.

ETHAN:
You are now the only person I actually know that does drag. [*Chulo looks at Serena.*]

SERENA:
Why Ethan, you don't like drag queens?

DANIEL:
The clubs are filled with drag queens.

ETHAN:
I didn't say I don't like drag queens. I just don't understand them. None of them were my friends until I met you. I've seen them at bars… Are you transgender?

SERENA:
No, not technically. Like most men, I couldn't handle hormone therapy. They made me an emotional basket case, bi polar. Happy one moment; on the warpath the next. I realized after a while that I enjoyed the smallest pleasures much more as a man, than I did when I was trying to medicate myself to be a woman. I love the feel of the cut of a silk blouse, the grace of a scarf, the fresh wisp of the scent of a woman…

CHULO:
Don't forget the shoes girl, don't forget the shoes.

DANIEL:
[To Serena] Are you married too?

SERENA:
Oh dear boy! I don't need someone to complete me. When I was young, I thought I had to have someone to complete me. After a life of realizing I had terrible judgment in boyfriends, I decided it was time to enjoy my own company, to learn to love myself enough to realize that being single did not mean I was alone.

DANIEL:
It must be nice knowing you get to plan out your own day without having to compromise your schedule with someone else.

SERENA:
I was willing to compromise a life. Unfortunately, the guys I chose didn't want compromise, they wanted submission.

ETHAN:
I don't think I could live with a drag queen.

CHULO:
Excuse me?

SERENA:
[Lets out a sharp, quick laugh.] Never?

ETHAN:
Never. I have a gay man's concept of drag queens.

DANIEL:
I picture them sitting around all day trying to figure out their music. Never being able to listen to the radio without them making every song with a female into a drag production from the front seat of the car.

ETHAN:
I grew up with sisters that trashed the bathroom with makeup, hairdryers, curling irons, hairspray, and so much clutter that the vanity was lost. Not to mention finding nail polish bottles rolling behind the toilet.

CHULO:
But they are creative.

ETHAN:
But it seems they use all their time creating drag, ignoring any life not drag related. I guess it would be a pretty lonely place for a guy dating a drag queen, if he had no interest in drag queens. I need to date someone that gives me equal relevance.

CHULO:
You are very important to me. You will always be my priority.

ETHAN:
Well, that is easy for you to say, you're not a drag queen.

SERENA:
[*Laughs.*] I never realized Ethan was so prejudiced. Were you not loved by your WYNTER?

ETHAN:
I have the best parents in the world. [*Daniel bows head and slouches into chair.*] Please, my dad was my best man at my wedding.

CHULO:
I love your parents.

SERENA:
My parents haven't included me in anything since I came out. They admit I was born. They even have my Army graduation photo from Ft. Knox on their fireplace mantle, but their yearly Christmas party with the other Providence Methodists will never include me. [*To Daniel.*] What about you Daniel, you still breast feeding at home from your mother?

CHULO:
[*Jumps up to run over to Daniel. Chulo sits in front of Daniel on the edge of the chair holding his hand.*] It's okay baby.

ETHAN:
[*Moving closer to Serena.*] She doesn't know Daniel, she didn't know...

SERENA:
Oh my, what have I stepped in now?

CHULO:
[*Slowly Chulo reaches down to use both of his hands to unroll the cuffs of Daniel's shirt. Lifts Daniel's arms.*] You are safe here honey.

SERENA:
I did not know. Oh goodness. You cut both arms?

ETHAN:
I just picked him up from the hospital this morning. They kept Daniel in for
a few days, because his father refused to sign him out.

CHULO:
[*Falls to his knees to hug Daniel. Daniel is starting to cry.*] Don't worry
baby, your father is not here to hurt you, you can call me Papi, everyone
calls me Papi.

SERENA:
Did his father cut him? [*Daniel pushes Chulo back up to the coffee table.
Daniel loudly sniff before he uses each sleeve one by one as a handkerchief
to wipe his nose.*]

DANIEL:
I told my father I was gay the night before my mother's birthday last week.
I lost my WYNTER three months ago; she was the only family that knew my
secret. She made me promise on her deathbed, past the morphine drip to
ease the pain from cancer, that I would tell my father I was gay before her
birthday, as a gift to her. I wasn't prepared emotionally, and I began crying.
I looked into my father's face. For the first time in my life, I saw tears in his
eyes. In my nervousness, I began to talk faster and he said nothing. I told
him I could not live without him by my side. He excused himself from the
table. A few minutes later, he came back into the kitchen telling me he
would not be staying in the house that night. As he opened the back door
to leave, he reached into his pocket, and placed in front of me... his gun.
[*Pause to let audience understand statement.*]

CHULO:
You know what darling, Serena there on the couch is staying at a hotel for
the next few weeks because she refuses to sleep on a couch, so this opens
the couch for you to crash on for a few weeks until we can help you get an
apartment.

SERENA:
I know you said you can do community theater, but do you have any other
skills to get a normal job that can pay your bills without living with your
father?

CHULO:
[*To Ethan.*] Where did you meet Daniel?

DANIEL:
Six Flags.

SERENA:
Six Flags?

ETHAN:
Near Springfield. Like he said, he is a dancer.

DANIEL:
[*To Serena.*] Like a real dancer, one that doesn't live off dollar bills.

SERENA:
Honey, I'm not cutting a paycheck down. I've been a drag queen living on
crumpled dollar bills my whole life, I just know as a fact, dollar bills are only
dollar bills. I still had my boy job until I retired early last year from Verizon.

CHULO:
She began at Verizon when they called it GTE. Auntie Serena used to be an
operator back in the day when they called him Jon Powers.

ETHAN:
Really, you were an operator?

CHULO:
When we were small puppies, Auntie Serena would practice her princess
voice on the phone, trying to get the customer to call him, "a her."

SERENA:
I finally discovered my normal voice was more natural than falsetto.
[*Mimic falsetto.*] Yes, sir that is Bassett, correct? I have listings of four Chris
Bassett's and two C. Bassett's. Perhaps you can assist me by telling me the
street where they live. No? Well, let me give you the first two numbers.
You can always call us back to get the other two. No problem, this is what
we do here at GTE. Yes sir, thank you sir. Good bye.

DANIEL:
[*Laughs. The tension in the room drops.*] I didn't know the operator used to
be a person. [*Everyone laughs.*]

SERENA:
Oh yes, there were many operators back in the day. We were like a family.

CHULO:
Speaking of family, there is a reason gay men and lesbians call each other family. For many of us, our friends became our family once we were rejected.

DANIEL:
But I don't like most of my friends.

ETHAN:
Then find better friends. You can't choose your family Daniel, but you can choose your friends.

SERENA:
Never be naïve to believe you have to like people defined as your family. I love my brother, but this does not make him my friend. One has nothing to do with the other. You can love your father, and still move on with your life. Remember the good parts he brought to your life, and push past the rest. The burden is his to carry not yours.

CHULO:
I say this all the time, if you focus on those around you that believe in you… you won't have the time to worry about others. Every moment you waste on people that don't believe in you, YOU steal from people that do believe in you Daniel.

ETHAN:
For the next few weeks, this will be your home. [*Ethan stands. Starts walking to the dining room table.*] You can help Serena and Chulo put all this craziness away while I'm at work.

SERENA:
Wait a second Daniel, so you can dance, dance?

DANIEL:
I love dancing. The park closed for the winter, and seconds later, I was laid off until spring. Four weeks later, my mom went in to Massachusetts General. She never left the hospital alive, and my father gave up hope for his own life. Six Flags isn't scheduled to re-open for three more weeks.

ETHAN:
I'm sure we can find something around here for you to do to help us out.

CHULO:
Let's stop thinking about your dad right now, until we can fix you. [*Chulo stands.*] You can help me put all of this away.

ETHAN:
[*Reading side of the large shoebox on the table. The box is so large, that he needs to stand on a chair to look inside.*] What is really in this box?

SERENA:
You were sent to us today.

DANIEL:
Excuse me?

SERENA:
[*Pulling Chulo's arm.*] Don't you get it Chulo, Daniel is here to rescue you. He was sent by an angel for both of you to rescue each other.

CHULO:
[*Looking at the mess.*] It's going to take more than three weeks to put all of this away. [*All of them are still ignoring Ethan. Ethan is now pulling out a chair to look inside the box.*]

ETHAN:
What is really inside this box?

DANIEL:
I can help unpack.

SERENA:
I'm not talking about cleaning up after Chulo, I'm talking about dancing.

ETHAN:
This is a pretty big box. [*Reading side.*] Shoes, Box one of three. What kind of man owns this many shoes? You have three boxes this size?

CHULO:
Serena, I think Wynter has found her dancer.

DANIEL:
You want me to strip for someone?

ETHAN:
[*Pulling duct tape from top of box.*] All this duct tape. Why didn't you use packing tape? Who uses duct tape to secure boxes?

SERENA:
No, Wynter is a drag queen. She's going to Drag World Nationals in two weeks to compete in Classics. You can be her dance partner.

ETHAN:
[*Pulls out bright red pump.*] Why is this box packed with women's shoes?

CHULO:
Wynter is supposed to win this year. It's in the cards.

SERENA:
[*To Ethan.*] The shoes and all these dresses belong to Wynter Storm, the drag queen.

DANIEL: I can do that.

ETHAN:
I don't understand, why does a drag queen have all her stuff packed into my home?

CHULO:
[*To Daniel.*] You'll have to practice hard the next two weeks.

ETHAN:
Hello! Why are there drag queen shoes and dresses all over this house?

DANIEL:
I can do that.

SERENA:
You'll get to travel to Nationals with Wynter to compete.

ETHAN:
[*Now screaming, pissed. Defines each word*] Who... is... Wynter? [*Almost falls off the chair, shaking the box.*]

DANIEL: Who is Wynter?

CHULO: I [Pause] am Wynter Storm.

SERENA:
[Running to catch Ethan from passing out.] Breathe Ethan, breathe.

[Close curtain. End of Act One.]

Act II Following Wynter
Scene One
Time: 40:00

> *Curtain opens. Boxes are no longer on stage. Stage is over-flowing with debris, dresses, shoes, and drag production props leaning across the back wall (over the painting). Daniel is sleeping on the couch with a blanket over him. Ensure the blanket's color is high contrast to the couch, so the audience can see Daniel moving under it without waking up. The lights are off. You can see a light coming from the bathroom and kitchen door. Pause ten seconds. The audience can see Daniel adjusting the pillows and his blanket. Room is quiet until the tenth second. On the tenth-second, we hear a loud crash in the bathroom followed by thirty seconds of Ethan screaming, glass breaking, and objects falling in the bathroom.*

CHULO:
[*Runs out of bedroom with a mask on his head used to block light. He is wearing obnoxious boxer underwear and a large wife beater tank top. He runs directly to the kitchen, assuming the noise is coming from the back door.*] Good God, call 9-1-1. Someone is breaking in through the back door, someone is breaking through the back door. [*As Chulo heads to the back door, he is carrying a foam head used for wigs like a bat.*] Call 9-1-1. Call 9-1-1… [*Stops at entrance to door, with his back to STAGE LEFT wall. Adjusts his crotch, puffs up his arms, and rushes into kitchen screaming. Noise starts up again with banging briefly on the bathroom door. Chulo cautiously exits kitchen Noise stops again. Chulo is walking to the front door with the wig head still above his head. Chulo stands in front of bathroom door staring at the front door.*] How can you not hear someone at the front door Daniel? [*As soon as Chulo says the word "Daniel," another loud bang comes from the bathroom door. Chulo turns around screaming, throwing the head towards the kitchen. Daniel, wearing underwear and a bright pink robe, cuffed in feathers, with "Storm" written on the back, jumps to his feet screaming. Both of them start screaming. Daniel does not know why he is screaming.*] Get the door! [*Chulo is pointing at the bathroom door.*]

DANIEL:
[*Still screaming.*] Why? What's inside the bathroom?

CHULO: I don't know. It's a wild animal.

DANIEL:
An animal? How did an animal get caught in the bathroom?

CHULO:
How do I know? I'm from Florida. Alligators are constantly crawling into our homes!

DANIEL:
Alligators? We live in downtown Boston. We don't have Alligators crawling down the streets of Boston.

CHULO:
I've heard stories about New York City. Perhaps it crawled in from the sewer. Maybe it's a deer!

DANIEL:
Honey, we don't have deer in downtown Boston. [*Suddenly another loud bang at the bathroom door.*]

ETHAN:
[*Screaming through the door.*] Shut up and open this door!

CHULO:
[*Screams again, running towards the kitchen table.*] Oh my God, the alligator crawled through the toilet.

DANIEL:
[*Rushing to bathroom.*] Someone's caught in the bathroom. It's a man's voice.

CHULO:
[*Turns facing bathroom door, holding up a chair like a lion tamer.*] What, an alligator chased a man out of the sewer and into our bathroom? [*Daniel cautiously opens bathroom door. Out stumbles Ethan. Both of his hands are above his head, each pointing in opposite awkward angles. A combination of pantyhose, bras, and neon colored clothesline with big wooden laundry clips are wound around him in a tangled mess. Ethan can barely walk out. Chulo screams again.*]

ETHAN:
[*Yelling.*] No one told me they were drying clothes in the bathroom.

DANIEL:
[*Realizing its Ethan, runs to untangle him.*] Ethan!

CHULO:
Oh it's Ethan. [*Helps Daniel untangle Ethan.*] I'm sorry. I was planning to put them away last night.

ETHAN:

Stop telling me what you are planning on doing. Unless it smells like hair spray, you have no interest. Look at this house. I tried so hard to make my home **OUR** home, to give you respect. In return, you made our home only **YOUR** home. I have to live here too.

DANIEL:

I can help clean today. I promise to help clean the house.

CHULO:

[Crosses stage to hug Ethan.] I'm sorry Ethan. I've been running around crazy the past two weeks. This pageant in Tampa means so much to me. Once it's over, I won't have so much drag stuff piled all over the house.

ETHAN:

[Reaches down. Pulls up a pudding cup with a spoon stuck inside the cup.] Pudding cups, Popsicle wrappers, candy wrappers, the remnants of every pastry in the Little Debbie line. It doesn't end Chulo. You are selfish. You are the only man I know that puts on a ribbed condom inside out for your own pleasure.

CHULO:

[Embarrassed. Rushes to grab cup.] I was planning on-

ETHAN:

[Interrupts Chulo.] Stop telling me that lie. I don't care about what you were planning on doing. What you say is not what you do. Your word is not your bond. I walk my talk Chulo. Everything I've told you I would do, I instantly did. You stole our home and kicked me out of it emotionally. This is not my safe place... ITS A PIGSTY. *[Chulo's head pops up scaring Daniel. Daniel runs in bathroom.]*

DANIEL:

Oh my, let me in here. *[Shutting door.]* I'll clean up after the alligator.

CHULO:

[Passive, repentant.] I won't repeat that I am sorry. I know the past two weeks I've said I'm sorry a thousand times and made no effort to change anything. I've always had my WYNTER living at home to clean up my room every day of the week.

ETHAN:

I have not found my cat Willow since you moved in. I can't be your WYNTER.

CHULO:
I don't want you to be my parent. I married you because you are strong. You give me emotionally what I need, and I never asked myself seriously, "If I was returning the blessing to you." *[Walks over. Grabs Ethan's hand to guide him to the couch.]* Sit down with me honey. If you can just bear with me one more day. Tonight when you come home, you will come home. We are loading up the moving van with the props and wardrobe for the drive to Tampa. All the rest of this I'll stick in the attic. We can make the entire attic my drag room. You won't have to see it any more.

ETHAN:
None of it?

CHULO:
Most of it.

ETHAN:
So lots of it will still be down here after you return?

CHULO:
Work with me here honey. I never promised you a rose garden.

ETHAN:
If I want a rose garden, I'll plant one outside. I don't understand, if you are only doing a few numbers, why does our place look like this?

CHULO:
It's a drag thing. The room inspires me. I lay it all out and let my imagination put it together.

ETHAN:
This room looks like a crime scene. And it looks like the cops are still hunting for clues after the burglars trashed the house.

CHULO:
[Pause. Scrunches face, not understanding correlation.] I'm thinking more poetically along the lines of an artist with a canvas. *[Knock at front door.]* That will be Serena with her Starbucks. *[Starts to stand but the bathroom door quickly opens. Daniel runs out.]* Plus I know Willow is still in here, because someone is eating her food.

ETHAN:
I wouldn't be surprised if it's a caravan of those nine pound Gambian pouch rats from Key West.

DANIEL:
I got it, I got it. *[Bursts out of room. Holding his left arm to signal everyone in the room to stop. Opens front door, still in his underwear.]* Hi Serena.

SERENA:
[Enters, slowly checking Daniel from head to toe. Serena is carrying a small clutch purse. Does not notice Chulo and Ethan on couch.] Stop, stop begging me for sex. Put on some damn drawers. Wait. *{Serena opens purse. Slowly removes cell phone. Takes picture.]* Okay darling you can go now. *[Daniel turns to walk to dining room table where his jeans and t-shirt are draped over the back of one of the dining room chairs. Serena takes a photo of Daniel's ass. Notices Chulo and Ethan. Shrugs.]* Hey, some nights are longer than other lonely nights.

ETHAN:
Good morning Serena. *[Stands. Kisses Serena before exiting to kitchen to make coffee.]* Chock Full of Nuts calls me.

DANIEL:
I didn't say anything.

CHULO:
[Stands, to Daniel.] It's the coffee.

DANIEL:
The coffee called him? I didn't hear anything. *[Walks into kitchen.]* Do we have any donuts left in the box? *[Exits to kitchen.]*

SERENA:
[To Daniel] I'm glad you got pretty down, because without it... you would starve to death. *[Crosses to hug Chulo.]* Why is everyone undressed? Don't you all believe in clothes in the morning? You're not barbarians. *[Hugs Chulo. Steps back. Takes another photo with cell phone.]* And why are you wearing that ridiculous outfit to bed?

CHULO:
What are you talking about? This is the same type of outfit I've worn to bed since I've known you. *[Screams to Ethan.]* Check Willow's litter box.

SERENA:
Papi, no wonder you've been single. You need to clean up this house and throw away those underwear. I'm surprised with Ethan's bad heart, that he can get excited enough to mess around with you. Wearing that outfit is like having a force field wrapped around you, screaming, "leave me alone, I need to sleep."

CHULO:
He doesn't need to get an erection. The doctors installed a tube he fills up inside of him with a pump.

SERENA:
Talk about, too much information.

CHULO:
Please, if I had one of them inside of mine, I would never let it down!
[Serena walks away offended, sits on STAGE RIGHT living room chair. Ethan enters with coffee. Sits at kitchen table.]

ETHAN:
Why does my cat have glitter in her poop? *[Serena and Chulo shrug shoulders.]* I don't understand why the three of you just don't fly to Tampa. We have enough large suitcases. *[Chulo bursts into a loud laugh.]*

SERENA:
For the record, Chulo has glitter in his poop. Hell, who am I kidding, he still poops out Mardi Gras beads. Plus, I will never fly with this lunatic again. *[Points to Chulo. Chulo is now laughing hysterically.]*

ETHAN:
I don't understand. Papi had no problem flying here to meet me the past few months.

SERENA:
He's not afraid to fly; I am. Chulo is an ass!

CHULO:
[Continues laughing. Explains to Ethan.] Serena refused to fly when we were growing up. About ten years ago, we had to fly back to Rhode Island for her father's funeral. The only way to get there on time, since we didn't own a car... was by plane.

SERENA:
I was freaked out.

CHULO:
The morning of the flight, she was being rude and belligerent.

SERENA:
I couldn't help myself Ethan. I was freaking out all night long.

CHULO:
Every two seconds Serena would make some off the cuff remark slamming me. By the time she sat down in her seat, she and I were in a full-blown fight.

SERENA:
You made me sit on the aisle.

CHULO:
[Brushing off comment.] Please letting you look outside would have been worse.

SERENA:
Nothing could have been worse.

CHULO:
[Continues story.] Serena would not shut up. [Chulo holds up fingers imitating Serena whining] Blah, blah, blah, blah. Nag, nag, nag, blah, blah.

SERENA:
The plane began to race down the runway as it prepared to take off.

CHULO:
I glanced over, wanting to spit on her for being so mean to me.

SERENA:
I was terrified, white as a ghost. I could feel my nails digging into the armrest. Out of the corner of my eye, I could see my best friend reaching up with his right hand to calm me.

CHULO:
I could tell Serena thought it was safe to put her wall down.

SERENA:
Chulo placed his hand on top of mine, and slowly squeezed it, as if to say... it's alright my friend.

CHULO:
[Bursts out laughing, jumping to his feet.] But I was actually using my pinky finger to disengage the seat button as the plane took off. [Chulo screams loudly.] Bamm! [Thrusts head backwards.] The force of the plane taking off slammed her headrest back so hard I thought the man behind her was going to break his nose jumping.

SERENA: I screamed!

CHULO:
[Now in overdrive of the conversation. He is imitating the scene in over-the-top gestures and sounds.] Blood curdling scream. [Chulo begins screaming.] Serena jumped out of her seat, screaming out at the top of her lungs as she ran the entire length of the plane to the toilet, "THE PLANE IS CRASHING, THE PLANE IS CRASHING, THE PLANE IS CRASHING." [Everyone is laughing.]

SERENA:
An ass! ...I was in the bathroom from Miami to JFK curled on the floor balling my eyes out, embarrassed to open the door until everyone departed the plane.

ETHAN:
So what happened?

CHULO:
Well, let's just say United Airlines made sure I understood the friendly skies would never include me as one of their passengers.

ETHAN:
[To Serena.] You must admit, the story is funny now.

SERENA:
As long as I don't EVER have to take another plane.

CHULO:
Please, those flight attendants are still repeating this story. [Mimicking again in almost a whisper, hands in the air. Sits on couch.] The plane is crashing, the plane is crashing. I had better save myself by hiding next to the toilet. [Daniel enters carrying a half donut. Sits next to Chulo.] Oh, I forgot we bought donuts. Go grab me one.

DANIEL:
This is the last one.

ETHAN:
[Laughs.] Daniel's teasing you. There are three doughnuts in the box.

DANIEL:
No seriously, I didn't realize you wanted a donut. This is the last one.

CHULO:
[Reaches over. Grabs donut to eat.] I think I liked you better when you were shy.

SERENA:

[Stands.] Thankfully, we packed everything in the van last night. We should bring an additional backup outfit for everything in your wardrobe.

ETHAN:

Can't you just pack needle and thread?

SERENA:

Needle and thread won't repair something lost along the way or a heel that breaks.

DANIEL:

It will repair a tear.

SERENA:

Please. I would have won a contest once in New Orleans, but I did a backflip and snagged my high heel on the back of my shirt tearing it in half.

CHULO:

I couldn't get my heel snagged in my blouse if I threw the heels on the floor and dragged my belly across it on the carpet.

SERENA:

[Stands up.] We need to walk through the routines a few more times before we leave. We're not going to be able to practice sitting in a van. [Serena walks over to the boom box sitting on the kitchen table. She turns. Realizes Chulo and Daniel are still seated. Cue music the instant she screams.] On your feet, on your mark! [Music is blaring. Ethan jumps up. He runs to the center of the room and stares up.]

ETHAN:

What the... [Turns to Chulo.] Where is my brand new ceiling fan?
I thought you said you were going to use this time to clean.

[Chulo pushes Ethan into CENTER STAGE chair. Chulo starts routine with Daniel. . Start song and music of your choice)

[Performs routine]

ETHAN:

[Stands. Walks back to kitchen.] I'm pretty confident I already put a damn ring on it. I have the pictures on facebook to prove it. [Sternly.] If you leave this mess for me to clean up today, than you will find it all crammed in the attic.

CHULO:

[Not understanding it is a threat. Chulo pretends it is an offer to help. Runs to Ethan, wrapping his arms around him, sarcastically sweet.] Thank you for offering to help me organize all of this in the attic. You are the greatest boyfriend ever. *[Chulo exits to bedroom.]* Ever!! Time to put some pants on. I keep noticing Daniel checking out my Kibbles and Bits. *[Looks at Daniel.]* Pervert! *[Exit to bedroom.]*

ETHAN:
[Trying to clarify his statement as he exits to kitchen.] I was being sarcastic. *[Pause.]* This is ridiculous. *[Exits to kitchen.]*

SERENA:
[Picks up box from next to couch. Crosses to bedroom door. Knocks.] Girl, open the door.

CHULO:
[Through closed door.] What do you want?

SERENA:
[Reads the sticker on the box.] WARNING: There are two containers you wish your family never opens. One is under my bed. This is the other one. *[Pause. Door slowly opens. Hands slowly reach to bring box back into the bedroom.]*

DANIEL:
I don't get it. What was in the box.

SERENA:
[Pause. Looking back at bedroom door.] It was the first time I actually got excited about the possibility of flying.

DANIEL:
Why? *[Ethan enters from kitchen.]*

SERENA:
I would have removed two of the toys from the box, wrapped a wire around it secured by a clock, and hid it in her damn carry-on suitcase.

ETHAN:
Who is she?

SERENA:
Wynter.

DANIEL:
Your wife.

ETHAN:
You drag queens confuse me. First, you tell me that you are only women on stage, and you claim you instantly become men again once you take off the face.

SERENA:
We do *[Matter-of-factly.]*

ETHAN:
But you don't. How many people call you Jonathon? How many people call Chulo only by her drag name? Neither of you correct them to say, "without a face, I am not a woman."

DANIEL:
A good point. I never thought of it that way. Plus… you constantly call each other, "her, she, woman, girl…"

SERENA:
Shut up and sit down Daniel. Look pretty.

ETHAN:
Why are you getting mad at Daniel? I think it's a fair question.

DANIEL:
I wasn't trying to be mean. This drag stuff now intrigues me.

ETHAN:
Now look what you've done. You're going to influence him to become a drag queen.

SERENA:
Please. This boy is a hop, skip, and a jump from a roll of duct tape and a case of Aqua Net. *[Chulo exits bedroom. He drags a massive chest suitcase on wheels similar to the cover of this script. The furniture is in his way.]*

DANIEL:
[Standing. Posing to Serena.] Really? I think I would look pretty in drag.

ETHAN:
[Rushes to move furniture. Takes handle from Chulo and maneuvers the chest next to the dining room table.] No wonder you are unable to fly in a plane. The last flight carrying something this large dropped out of an army plane over England.

DANIEL:
I thought you said you were in Britain.

SERENA:
[Laughs.] Do you think Britain is a country?

DANIEL:
Yes. I'm not illiterate. Britain is in between Italy and Europe.

ETHAN:
[Laughs.] Which people live in the country called Europe.

DANIEL:
I know you all are trying to stump me, but I'm on my game this morning. I have my thinking cap on. [Pauses. Taps his head with his second finger.] Europeans of course! [The entire room stats laughing at Daniel. Daniel looks proud knowing he had the correct answer.] See, I'm not just another pretty boy.

SERENA:
You may want to carry condoms Daniel. No sense getting yourself pregnant.

DANIEL:
[Puzzled.] My pants are too tight.

CHULO:
For condoms?

DANIEL:
For lube.

ETHAN:
[Embarrassed by the conversation.] You all talk about the most embarrassing stuff all the time.

SERENA:
Why would sex be embarrassing? We're not being vulgar. Are you old fashioned, believing it should be kept in the confines of your bedroom, in the dark, quietly done under the sheets?

ETHAN:
Well, actually... Yes!

CHULO:
Ethan is very conservative.

DANIEL:
I'm not going to let someone use just anything that is a gel. My last boyfriend hurt me after he convinced me that hair gel was the same as lubricant.

SERENA:
Chulo has you all beat.

CHULO:
Shut up Serena.

SERENA:
In the early eighties, her boyfriend ran in the kitchen looking for a quick fix to his session with Chulo. He grabbed my new Crisco from the grocery bags without me noticing. I was pissed. Here I am trying to make this new cookie recipe and I couldn't figure out where my new package disappeared to.

CHULO:
Shut up Serena.

SERENA:
It was a new product called Butter flavored Crisco. About an hour later in walks the very messy and disheveled Wynter Storm reeking of the smell of butter.

CHULO:
Shut up Serena.

SERENA:
She tried lying that it wasn't them that stole the container; not that I wanted it back! For months, and I truly state months... we all walked around Key West calling her Molly McButterbutt! *[The entire room bursts into laughter.]*

CHULO:
I could have killed Serena. Talk about having Instant Messaging before the term was even invented.

SERENA:
I was pissed you took my Crisco.

CHULO:
You are so full of it. I personally watched her tell this story a dozen times the first week alone. Every time she told the story, her smile got larger and the laughter became louder. Within days, I believe show hosts at the local bars were sharing the story on stage.

SERENA:
You were always a mess back in the day. *[To Daniel.]* If we turn you into a drag queen, make sure it's something nice. Chulo was such a mess. We were trying to think of a name for him. Wynter Wonderland, Wynter Breeze, Wynter Carnival, she was so stuck on the name Wynter.

CHULO:
"God is in my head, but the devil is in my pants." It's a quote from comedian Jonathan Winters. I loved him growing up. He once said, "If your ship doesn't come in, swim out to meet it." It hit home with me. I was so crazy growing up.

SERENA:
She was a mess. We had to name her Wynter Storm, because "*Wynter Are you kidding me with all this stupid crap girl*"... just seemed too long to remember.

DANIEL:
I don't want to be a mess *[Sits on couch. Covers himself with the two pillows and blanket. Looks very insecure again]*.

SERENA:
Only you can make that judgment call. Having an "I don't care what other people think" attitude only leads to an ugly place. Be wise. Weak people replace confidence with arrogance.

CHULO:
A couple of the performers in the competition are arrogant. I'm not saying they don't have talent. If they didn't have talent, they wouldn't be in the show, but even the prettiest person looks ugly with bitterness stained on their face.

DANIEL:
Do they all have crowns from other pageants?

CHULO:
No. Drag World covers the entertainers that never won a national title from one of the big systems.

ETHAN:
I went on facebook and looked them all up. Most of them had crowns.

SERENA:
So many pageants with so many crowns. At this point I think they hand you a crown at the 7-11 with a Slurpee.

DANIEL:
[Picks up wig head. Wig falls to floor. He quickly picks up the wig. To Chulo.] Sorry.

SERENA:
[Laughs.] Please. The last time I lost that much hair I was standing in the shower.

CHULO:
We have to get on the road in a few minutes. I'm so nervous. *[To Ethan.]* I'm falling to pieces!

SERENA:
With all that Aqua Net on your head all day long, it won't fall far!

CHULO:
Ha ha. You won't be laughing when we get there and Big Bertha Bovine is staring you down.

DANIEL:
Who is Big Bertha Bovine?

ETHAN:
Big Bertha Bovine?

SERENA:
From Columbus, Ohio. She lost to me the year I won. She's been bitter ever since.

CHULO:
She's three-hundred pounds, but boy can she dance!

SERENA:
Are you kidding me? She can't dance for her life. She's lucky if she can make bus fare.

CHULO:
So not true. Plus, your drag mother will be at this year's competition.

SERENA:
She's not my drag mother anymore.

DANIEL:
Who is your drag mother?

SERENA:
Was... WAS my drag WYNTER. She moved to Phoenix and stopped talking to me years ago after I changed my drag name to Serena.

ETHAN:
What did it used to be?

DANIEL:
Why would she care?

CHULO:
[To Ethan.] Gypsy Rose, because she constantly moved like a gypsy when she was younger.

SERENA:
Most performers get part of their name from their mentors or drag parents. By the time I settled down, I considered Gypsy derogatory to a couch surfer.

ETHAN:
What is a couch surfer?

CHULO:
A homeless bum. Someone not responsible enough to pay his own bills, so he crashes from one couch to another expecting other people to pay his way.

DANIEL:
[Covers head.] Oh great. I'm a couch surfer.

SERENA:
[Pulls blanket off Daniel's head. Places it on the other end of the couch.]
Don't be silly Daniel. You're doing something to help Wynter. *[Walks over to Chulo. Matter-of-factly.]* I became a respectable woman. I needed a real name.

CHULO:
She loved wearing silver jewelry in the seventies and eighties.

ETHAN:
And Serena?

SERENA:
We were trying to be clever. Serena is the alter ego of Samantha on the television show, "Bewitched."

CHULO:
[Trying to explain to a puzzled Daniel.] The kooky cousin. Looked exactly like the blonde-haired person, Elizabeth Montgomery, because it was Elizabeth Montgomery in a black wig acting wicked. *[Daniel shrugs still puzzled.]*

ETHAN:
"Bewitched," the television show?

SERENA:
For Christ's sake Daniel, didn't mom and dad have Nick at Night on your TV set? Even I know who Milton Berle is and he wasn't during my generation.

DANIEL:
I know who Milton Berle is… Why do you all talk to me like I was born yesterday. My mom's favorite brown purse is a Milton Berle bag.

CHULO:
[Burst out laughing.] A Milton Berle?

ETHAN:
Milton Berle made handbags?

SERENA:
She doesn't have a Milton Berle handbag.

CHULO:
What is a Milton Berle hand bag?

SERENA:
He's referring to a Louis Vuitton. *[Everyone laughs.]* Daniel. If you decide to perform drag, you can have my drag mother as your own.

DANIEL:
[Sarcastically. Clapping quickly.] Oh goody. I am so damn excited. Not only is she my new drag WYNTER, but she is the only drag queen to have ever won the Miss Church's Chicken Pageant three years in a row. *[Chulo laughs. Walks DOWNSTAGE CENTER to pick up his shoes.]*

SERENA:
With that said, Daniel we are out the door. Let's give our two love birds a few minutes to say goodbye and kiss and all that old gross stuff that only looks sexy when done by hot, sexy hunks.

DANIEL:
[Tosses pillows to other end of couch. Jumps up. Embarrassed. Shyly.] So, do you think I would look sexy making out?

SERENA:
[Looks at him head to toe.] Depends. *[Walks to front door. Opens it for Daniel to exit.]*

DANIEL:
On what? *[Exits front door.]*

SERENA:
[To Chulo and Ethan.] Who you are kissing, is it me, and are you talking.

DANIEL:
[Off stage.] You would really kiss me.

SERENA:
Only if it will make you shut up. *[Shuts door.]*

CHULO:
[Turns to Ethan. Ethan crosses room to meet CENTER DOWNSTAGE.] If that boy ever did drag, I think his name would still have to be Powder Puff.

ETHAN:
I'm going to miss you Papi.

CHULO:
[Points around the room.] All of me?

ETHAN:
[Pats Chulo's belly.] All of you. [Points around the room.] This crap will be crammed in the attic by the time you get back.

CHULO:
[Sincerely. Affectionately.] You are such a kind man Ethan Evans. I wouldn't blame you for cramming all of this into a trash bag and tossing it up there.

ETHAN:
I will make you a promise, [Hugging Chulo.] I'm going to build a floor, shelves, and racks in the attic. You will be pretty proud of your work space considering the attic is as large as the entire house.

CHULO:
I believe you. [Rests his head on Ethan's shoulder, facing audience.] Thank you Ethan. I've been such a tornado since I moved in two weeks ago. I bet you haven't had a chance to tell me anything about yourself because it's been about me, me, me. I promise, as soon as I get home I will make it up to you. No more secrets. [Looks up into Ethan's eyes. Speaking slowly.] I promise. No more secrets. We've both proved to each other that there is nothing that we can hide that will destroy us. Right?

ETHAN:
[Quickly kisses Chulo.] Right. No secrets will ever break us up.

CHULO:
[Pulls away.] Oh dear, I need to potty one more time before we leave. Will you bring out my suitcase? [Exits quickly into bathroom.]

ETHAN:
Yes dear. [Pause. Count to five. Walks to suitcase. Amazed by its size. Looks at the audience.] No secret will break us up. You all heard him say that ladies and gentleman. No secrets will break us up. A tornado indeed. [Pause.] Couldn't get a word in edge wise. Not a single word, not even to share my own secret. [Pause. Stops. Walks over to the apron of the stage. Whispers to audience.] No secret will break us up. Gosh. Wait until Wynter Storm realizes... [Pause.] I was born a girl. [Bathroom door opens. Chulo enters.]

CHULO:
Let's go baby. You going to follow me?

ETHAN:
[Struggling to pull suitcase.] Yes dear. Following Wynter. *[Both exit door. Door opens again. Ethan raises hands to wave to audience. Door shuts. Stage lights off.]*

Close curtain.
END OF PLAY

Ten Black Books

Book 1   DRAG411's
"DRAG Bully, A Survivor's Guide"

The Largest Bullying Project in LGBT History for Struggling Entertainers. Advice from over a hundred male, female, and androgynous impersonators around the world to help entertainers struggling with their family, peers, relationships, neighbors, regular jobs, venues, and successfully overcoming self-doubt. Best Selling author Todd Kachinski Kottmeier created DRAG411 to document the lives of male, female, and androgynous impersonator years ago. It is now the largest organization for impersonators on earth with over 7,000 entertainers in 32 countries. DRAG411 also operates The International Original, Official DRAG Memorial with almost a thousand names (2018). This is his 25th book, 20th World Record, and 12th book on this subject. Thousands of Invitations to contribute were send out. This book contains the best of their responses, in their own words, to you.

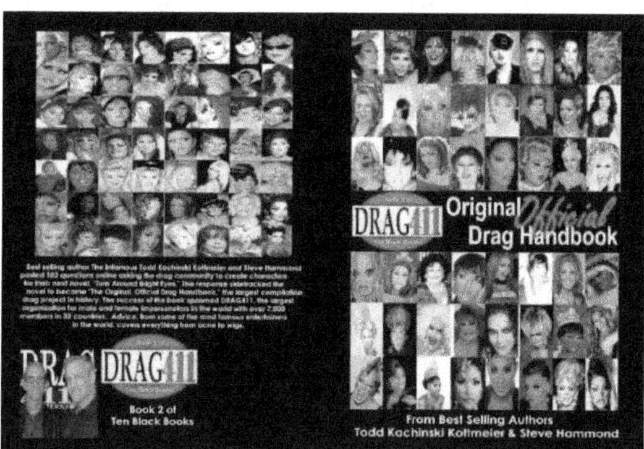

Book 2 DRAG411's
"Original DRAG Handbook"

Over 155 female impersonators (and 1 male impersonator) from around the world share over a thousand insightful comments in the first handbook created of this art form.

Commentary shared with Todd Kachinski

Kottmeier included the following contributors of The Original, DRAG Handbook to include Ada Buffet, Adora , Adrian Leigh, Afeelya Bunz, Alisa Summers, Alanna Divine, Alexis De La Mer, Alexis Mateo, Alex Serpa, Allure, Amanda Bone, Amanda Love, Amy DeMilo, Anastaia Fallon, Astasnaia Rexia, Angel gLamar, Angela Dodd, Anita Cox, April Fresh, Ashleigh Cooley, Aurora Sexton, Babette Schwartz, Bailey St. James, Barbra Herr, Barbra Seville, Beverly LaSalle, BJ Stephens, Blair Michaels, Brandon M. Caten, Brianna Lee, Brittany Moore, Brookyln Bisette, Bukkake Blaque London St. James, Cartier Paris, Cathy Craig, Champagne T. Bordeaux, Cherry Darling, Christina Paris, CoCo LaBelle, CoCo Montrese, CoCo St. James, Conundrum, Crystal Belle, Daniel Murphy, Danika Fierce, Daphne Ferraro, Dasha Nicole, Dee Gregory, Deva DaVyne, Diamond Dunhill, Diedra Windsor Walker, Dmentia Divinyl/Eva LaDeva, Echo Dazz, Esme Russell, Estelle Rivers, Eunyce Raye, Felica Fox, Felina Cashmere, Geraldine Queen Cabaret, Ginger Minj, Glitz Glam, Gilda Golden, Horchata, Ima Twat, Ineeda Twat, Jade Daniels, Jade Jolie, Jade Shanell, Jade Sotomayo, Jaeda Fuentes, Jami Micheals, Jay Santana, Jeffrey Powell, Jenna Chambers Tisdale, Jessica Jade, Jocelyn Summers, Jodie Holliday, Joey Brooks, Joshua Myers, J.P. Patrick, Juwanna Jackson, Kamden Wells, Katrina Starr, Kenny Braverman, Khrystal Leight, Kier Sarkesian, Kiki LaFlare Santangilo, Kitty D'Meaner, Kori Stevens, Krystal Amore Adonis, Lacey Lynn Taylors, Lady Clover Honey, Lady Sabrina, Lady TaJma Hall, Lakeisha Pryce, LeeAnna Love, Leigh Shannon, Lisa Carr, Lola Honey, Madisyn De La Mer, Makayla Rose Devine, Maxine Padlock (Maxi Pad), Melissa Morgan, Melody Mayheim, Michael Wilson, Mike Astermon-Glidden, Mis Sadistic, Miss Conception, Miss Gigi, Mr. Kenneth Blake, Misty Eyez, Monique Michaels, Myah Monroe, Mystique Summers, Nairobi V. D'Viante, Naomi D-Lish, Naomi Wynters, Nicole Paige Brooks, Nikki Dynamite, Nova Starr, Ororo, Patrica Grand, Patricia Knight, Patrica Mason, Pandora DeStrange, Penelope Reigns, Polly FunkChanel, Phiore Star Liemont, Purrzsa Kyttyn, Pussy LeHoot, Raquel Payne, Rhyana Vorhman, Rickie Lee, Rusti Fawcett, Scarlett Fever, Selina Kyle, Shae Shae LaReese, Shealita Babay, Shugah Caine, Stephanie Roberts, Stephanie Stuart, Stormy Vain, Summer Breeze, Sybil Storm, Tabatha Lovall, Tatum Michelle, Teri Courtney, Tiffani Middlesexx, Timm McBride, Toni Davyne, TotiYanah Diamond,Trixie LaRue, Trixie Pleasures, Vegas Platinum, Venus D Lite, Vivika D'Angelo, Wendel Duppert and Wendy G. Kennedy.

Book 3:   DRAG411's
"Crown Me! Winning Pageants"

Hundreds of invitations sent to the titleholders, pageant promoters, judges, and talent show hosts to share their insight on not only winning pageants and contests but also owning the stage every time they perform. Their topics included auxiliary steps to success needed for song selection, dancing, movement on stage, props, backup dancers, creating your own edge, personal interviews, steps to success for winning the talent category every time you step on stage, on stage questions, eveningwear, and creative costuming. They discussed in their own unedited words, wardrobe changes, makeup, hair, shoes, when is the time to compete, qualities needed for a judge, and the top misconceptions of contestants competing in the pageantry systems.

Commentary shared with Todd Kachinski Kottmeier included the following contributors of Crown Me! to include AJ Menendez, Amy Demilo, Anastacia Dupree, Anson Reign, Bob Taylor, Breonna Tenae, Brittany T Moore, Coco Montrese, Dana Douglas, Darryl Kent, Denise Russell, Dey Jzah Opulent, Freddy Prinze Charming, Gage Gatlyn, Jay Santana , Jayden Knight, Jennifer Foxx, Joey Jay, Kori Stevens, Mis Sadistic, Mykul Jay Valentine, Natasha Richards, Rico Taylor, Sam Hare, Stephanie Stuart, Taina T. Norell, Tiffani Middlesexx, Tori Taylor, Ty Nolan, Vinnie Marconi, and Vivika D'Angelo.

Book 4:   DRAG411's
"DRAG King Guide"

Over 155 male impersonators around the world share over a thousand insightful comments in forty-one chapters.

Commentary shared with Todd Kachinski Kottmeier included the following contributors of The Official DRAG King and Male Impersonators Guide to include Aaron Phoenix, Abs Hart, Adam All, Adam DoEve, AJ Menendez, Alec Allnight, Alexander Cameron, Alik Muf, Andrew Citino, Anjie Swidergal, Anson Reign, Ashton The Adorable Lover, Atown, Ayden Layne, B J Armani, B J Bottoms, Bailey Saint James, Ben Doverr, Ben Eaten, Bootzy Edwards Collynz, Brandon KC Young-Taylor, Bruno Diaz, Cage Masters, Campbell Reid Andrews, Chance Wise, Chandler J Hart, Chasin Love, Cherry Tyler

Manhattan, Chris Mandingo, Clark Kunt, Clint Torres, Cody Wellch Klondyke, Colin Grey, Corey James Caster, Coti Blayne, Crash Bandikok, Dakota Rain, Dante Diamond, Davion Summers, DeVery Bess, Devin G. Dame, Devon Ayers, Dionysus W Khaos, Diseal Tanks Roberts, D-Luv Saviyon, Dominic Demornay, Dominic Von Strap, D-Rex, Dylan Kane, E. M. Shaun, Eddie C. Broadway, Emilio, Erick LaRue, Flex Jonez, Freddy Prinze Charming, Gabe King, Gage Gatlyn, George De Micheal, Greyson Bolt, Gunner Gatlyn, Gus Magendor, Hawk Stuart, Harry Pi, Holden Michael, Howie Feltersnatch, Hurricane Savage, J Breezy St James, Jack E. Dickinson, Jack King, Jake Van Camp, Jamel Knight, Jenson C. Dean, Johnnie Blackheart, Jonah Godfather of DRAG, Jordan Allen, Jordan Reighn, Joshua K. Mann, Joshua Micheals, Juan Kerr, Julius M. SeizeHer, Jude Lawless, Justin Cider, Justin Luvan, Justin Sider, K'ne Cole, Kameo Dupree, Kenneth J. Squires, King Dante, King Ramsey, Jack Inman, Kody Sky, Koomah, Kristian Kyler, Kruz Mhee, Linda Hermann-Chasin, Luke Ateraz, Lyle Love-It, Macximus, Marcus Mayhem, Marty Brown, Master Cameron Eric Leon, Max Hardswell, MaXx Decco, Michael Christian, Mike Oxready, Miles Long, Mr-Charlie Smith, Nanette D'angelo Sylvan, Nolan Neptune, Orion Blaze Browne, Owlejandro Monroe, Papa Cherry, Papi Chulo, Papi Chulo Doll, Persian Prince, Phantom, Pierce Gabriel, Rasta Boi Punany, Rico M Taylor, Rock McGroyn, Rocky Valentino, Rogue DRAG King, Romeo Sanchez, Rychard "Alpha" Le'Sabre, Ryder Knightly, Ryder Long, Sam Masterson, Sammy Silver, Santana Romero, Scorpio, Shane Rebel Caine, Shook ByNature, Silk Steele Prince, SirMandingo Thatis, Smitty O'Toole, Soco Dupree, Spacee Kadett, Starr Masters, Stefan LeDude, Stefon Royce Iman, Stefon SanDiego, Stormm, Teddy Michael, Thug Passion, Travis Luvermore, Travis Hard, Trey C. Michaels, Trigger Montgomery, Tyler Manhattan, Viciouse Slick, Vinnie Marconi, Welland Dowd, William Vanity Matrix, Wulf Von Monroe, Xander Havoc, and Xavier Bottoms.

Book 5:   DRAG411's
"DRAG Stories"

Funny stories shared with Todd Kachinski Kottmeier including the following contributors of DRAG Stories to include Chance Wise, Anson Reign, Tiffani Middlesexx, Rico Taylor, Todd Kachinski Kottmeier, Bob Taylor, Stefon Royce Iman, Candi Samples, Alexis Mateo, Naomi Wynters, Dmentia Divinyl, Bruce Lacie, Kennedy Wendy, Chastity Rose, Miss GiGi, Angel gLamar, Patricia Grand, Shook ByNature, Lady Guy, Eunyce Raye, Charley Marie Coutora, Jezzie Bell, Lamar Kellam, Jayden St. James, Rachelle Ann Summers, Champagne T Bordeaux, Gilda Golden, Daisha Monet, Vivika D'Angelo, Rachel Boheme, Esme Rodriguez, and MaNu Da Original.

Book 6:   DRAG411's
"DRAG Mother, DRAG Father" Honoring Mentors

Performers look to DRAG mothers, DRAG fathers, friends, and fans for insight, compassion, and guidance as mentors. This book honors those special people. Over 140 entertainers contributed wisdom and words for this historical book, making it the largest project of its nature in GLBTQ history and the first published book on male and female mentors.

Commentary shared with Todd Kachinski Kottmeier included the following contributors of DRAG Parents to includee AJ Menendez, Vinnie Marconi, Mis Sadistic, Todd Kachinski Kottmeier, Bob Taylor, Taina Norell, Andrew Stratton, Horchata Horchata, David Warner, Gianna Love, Trinity Taylor, Domunique Jazmin Vizcaya, Brittany Moore, PurrZsa Kyttyn, Jake Lickus, Shelita Taylor, Adriana Manchez, MiMi Welch, China Taylor, Armondis Bone't, Monique Trudeau, Simeon Codfish, Diamond Dupree, Stefon Royce Iman, Jayden Stjames, Demonica da Bomb, Colin Grey, Christopher Todd Guy, Celyndra Lashay Clyne, Candice St. James, Justin Barnes Williams, Ivanna Dooche, London Taylor Douglas, Christina Alexandria Victoria Regina Lowe, Bianca DeMonet, Critiqa Mann, Jazmen Andrews, AJ Allen, TotiYanah Diamond, D' Marco Knight, Chip Matthews, Mirage Montrese, India Starr Simms, Jade S Stratton, Emerald Divine, Elysse Giovanni, Vanity Halston, Kristofer Reynolds, Akasha Uravitch, Adriana Fuentes, Erykah Mirage, Felicity Ferraro, Joey Payge, Rhiannon Todd, Vicious Slick, Amirage Saling, Tori Sass, Chy'enne Valentino, and Robbi Lynn.

Book 7:   DRAG411's
"Spotlight Today"

It was the World's Largest Paperback Magazine for Impersonators and Fans when it premiered with over 175 pages. DRAG411 no longer prints Spotlight Today Magazine, but here is the re-release of the groundbreaking first edition. Complete articles by Vinnie Marconi, Denise Russell, Tiffani T. Middlesexx, Kristofer Reynolds, Magenta Alexandria Dupree, Butch Daddy, Vivikah Kayson-Raye, Makanoe, Amanda Lay, Thomas DeVoyd, Kevin B. Reed, Glenn Storm, and over 150 impersonators from around the world.

Book 8:   DRAG411's
"DRAG Queen Guide"

Almost two hundred female impersonators around the world share over a thousand insightful comments in forty-one chapters.
Commentary shared with Todd Kachinski Kottmeier included the following contributors of Official DRAG Queen and Female Impersonator Handbook to include Alana Summers, Alexis Marie Von Furstenburg, Alize', Aloe Vera, Alysin Wonderland, Amanda Bone DeMornay, Amanda Lay, Amanda Roberts, Amy DeMilo, Anastasia Fallon, Angie Ovahness, Anita Mandinite, Appolonia Cruz, Ashlyn Tyler, Aurora Tr'Nele Michelle, Azia Sparks, Barbie Dayne, Barbra Herr, Beverly LaSalle, Bianca DeMonet, Bianca Lynn Breeze, Blair Michaels, Boxxa Vine, Brittany T Moore, Britney Towers, Brandi Amara Skyy, Brooke Lynn Bradshaw, Candi Samples, Candi Stratton, Candy

Sugar, Cathy Craig, Catia Lee Love, CeCe Georgia, Cee-Cee LaRouge-Avalon, Celeste Starr, Chad Michaels, Chevon Davis, Cheyenne Desoto Mykels, Chi Chi Lalique, Christina Collins, Chrystal Conners, Claudia B Eautiful, Coca Mesa, Coco St James, Damiana LaRoux, Dana

Scrumptious, Danyel Vasquez, Dee Gregory, Delores T. Van-Cartier, Demonica DaBaum, Denise Russell, Diamond Dunhill, Diva Lilo, Diva Savage, Dove, EdriAna Treviño, Elle Emenopé, Elysse Giovanni, Erica James, Esmé Rodríguez, Estella Sweet, Eunyce Raye, Eva Nichole Distruction, Faleasha Savage, Felicia Minor, Felicity Frockaccino, Gigi Masters, Ginger Alley, Ginger Gigi Diamond, Ginger Kaye Belmont, Glitz Glam, Grecia Montes D' Occa, Heather Daniels, Hennessy Heart, Hershae Chocolatae, Holy McGrail, Hope B Childs, Horchata, India Brooks, India Ferrah, Ivy Profen, Izzy Adahl, Jaclyn St James, Jade Iroq, Jade Sotomayor, Jade Taylor Stratton, Jamie-Ree Swan, Jennifer Warner, Jessica Brooks, Jexa Ren'ae Van de Kamp, Joey Brooks, Jonny Pride, Kamelle Toe, Karma Jayde Addams, Kelly Turner, Mama Savannah Georgia, Mr. Kenneth Blake, Kamden T. Rage, Kira Stone-St James, Kirby Kolby, Kita Rose, Krysta Radiance, Lacie Bruce, Lady Jasmine Michaels, Lady Pearl, Lady Sabrina, Latrice Royale, LaTonga Manchez, Leona Barr, Lexi Alexander, Lilo Monroe, Lindsay Carlton, Lucinda Holliday, Lunara Sky, Lupita Chiquita Michaels Alexander, Madam Diva Divine, Mahog Anny, Makayla Michelle Davis Diamond, Mariah Cherry, Maxine Padlock, Melody Mayheim, Menaje E'toi, Mercede Andrews, Mi$hal, Mia Fierce, Michelle Leigh Sterling, Miss Diva Savage, Miss GiGi, Misty Eyez, Mitze Peterbilt, Monica Mystique, Montrese Lamar Hollar, Morgana DeRaven, Muffy Vanbeaverhousen, Natasha Richards, Nathan Loveland, Nicole Paige Brooks, Nikki Garcia, Nostalgia Todd Ronin, Olivia St James, Paige Sinclair, Pandora DeCeption, Pheobe James, Reia'Cheille Lucious, Robyn Demornay, Robyn Graves, Rhonda Sheer, Rose Murphy, Ruby Diamond NY, Ruby Holiday, Ryan Royale, Rychard "Alpha" Le'Sabre, Rye Seronie, Sable Monay, Sabrina Kayson-Raye, Samantha St Clair, Sanaa Raelynn, Sapphire T. Mylan, Sasha Phillips, Savannah Rivers, Savannah Stevens, Selina Kyle, Sha'day Halston-St James, ShaeShae LaReese, Shamya Banx, Shana Nicole, Shaunna Rai, Sierra Foxx White, Sierra Santana, Sonja Jae Savage, Stella D'oro, Strawberry Whip, Sugarpill, Tasha Carter, Tanna Blake, Taquella Roze, Tawdri Hipburn, Taylor Rockland, Tempest DuJour, Tiffani T. Middlesexx, Traci Russell, Trudy Tyler, Vanessa del Rey, Velveeta WhoreMel, Vera Delmar, Vicky Summers, Vita DeVine, Vivian Sorensin, Vivian Von Brokenhymen, Vivika D'Angelo-Steele, Wendy G. Kennedy, Willmuh Dickfit, Wynter Storm, Yasmine Alexander and ZuZu Bella.

Book 9:   DRAG411's (Two Comedy Scripts)
"Best Said Dead" and **"Following Wynter"**

Best Said Dead examines in funny conversations those brief minutes after a person dies. Many religions and beliefs define different paths for each of us. Rarely do we discuss those precious moments between death and the final destination. This comedy opens the possibilities that for a moment, a person vanishes into the memories in their mind. Any part can be male, female, or ambiguous.

Following Wynter is a hilarious comedy play. Ethan discovers his newlywed husband is the flamboyant DRAG queen Wynter Storm in this whimsical farce with an important message of believing in yourself and your friends. . . even if your friend is Serena Silver. Any part can be male, female, or ambiguous.

Book 10:   DRAG411's
"DRAG World"
The contributing writers of DRAG411's "Spotlight Magazine," the World's Largest Paperback Magazine for Impersonators and Fans when it premiered in 2012 with over 175 pages, created this companion book. DRAG411 no longer prints Spotlight Today Magazine, but above you will find Book 7 is the re-release of the groundbreaking first edition. Complete chapters on DRAG Marketing by DRAG411.

Complimentary articles on Confidence, Duct Tape, Music Selection, Living Divinely, authentic stage presence, Pageants, having fun performing, jewelry, legislative information from the United States and around the world, the Old School performers, Virgin stage performers, and payday from contributing writers including Denise Russell, Jay Santana, Chance Wise, Vivikah Kayson-Raye, AJ Menedez, Glenn Storm, Freddy Prinze Charming, Gage Gatlyn, Kevin B. Reed, and over 100 impersonators from around the world!

Other books from the Best Selling author
The Infamous Todd Kachinski Kottmeier

"Turn Around Bright Eyes, The DRAG Queen Killer"

Few crimes in gay history rocked a nation as great as The DRAG Queen Killer. The country seemed paralyzed from the first ring of the chain tapping on the concrete, as they pulled Cassandra to her death, until the very last brutal killing. The murderous rampage seemed buried amongst the media suffering from a barrage of tales from the 9-11 terrorist attacks.

"CommUnity of Transition"

We sent over a thousand invitations to the transgender community around the world asking them to share wisdom, advice, and compassion for those questioning or struggling. No restraints, using topics they created, as they guided the conversation over forty chapters and fifty topics. By the close, these remarkable people had created the largest compilation book in transgender history. They opened their heart with these words.

NOTE: *This book is "lightly edited" to reflect the intent and form of over one hundred transgender contributors. Unedited photographs "before and after" come from actual contributing transgender writers.*

"Joey Brooks, The Show Must Go On"
By Joey Brooks and Todd Kachinski Kottmeier

Joey Brooks, The Show Must Go On is the story of The First Lady of Ybor from the days of El Goya to present day. Female Impersonator, Show director, hostess, author…

"Old school, new school, no school… who gives a shit? I'm too old to go to school. I barely remember last week. When I get too old to remember what the fuck I did when I was young …ger, I'll just open one of these books and laugh my ass off. I wonder how many other queens had this much fun becoming one of the icons of their community. Too funny. I just called myself an icon. Hell, I must be a queen. Only a female impersonator could call themselves a diva, a queen, a star without people giggling behind her back. Giggling is good. A twenty-dollar bill is better."

"Two Days Past Dead"

The Author's First Published Book

It is hard to be the good guy when you succeed so well being bad. This is the Auggie Summer's dilemma his entire life. The story, based loosely on the tales of The Infamous Todd, follows the precocious child. His story begins with selling candy in 9th grade where he catches not only the attention of the press but also amusement of the drug cartel early in its' own infancy. Auggie Summers finds himself in the forefront of one of the most dangerous organizations on Earth.

"Waiting On God"
The Author's Humorist Novel

Learn to live after the doctors tell you "that are dying." A humorist essay on embracing funny moments and to create an environment around you that makes people not only laugh, but also be inspired by your strength.

www.ingramcontent.com/pod-product-compliance
Lightning Source LLC
Chambersburg PA
CBHW070129260726
48658CB00001B/330